a
church
truly
catholic

a
church
truly
catholic

James K. Mathews

 ABINGDON PRESS
Nashville and New York

Scripture quotations noted RSV are from the Revised Standard Version of the Bible, copyrighted 1946 and 1952 by the Division of Christian Education, National Council of Churches, and are used by permission.

Scripture quotations noted NEB are from the New English Bible, New Testament. © the Delegates of the Oxford University Press and the Syndics of the Cambridge University Press 1961. Reprinted by permission.

The quotations by W. H. Auden are from "For the Time Being," in *The Collected Poetry of W. H. Auden*, copyright 1945. Used by permission of the publishers, Random House, Inc. and Faber and Faber, Ltd.

The lines by Robert Frost are from *A Masque of Reason* by Robert Frost. Copyright 1945 by Robert Frost. Reprinted by permission of Holt, Rinehart and Winston, Inc.

Some of the material in Chap. 4 appeared previously in an article by the author in *World Outlook* in 1966. Used by permission.

SET UP, PRINTED, AND BOUND BY THE
PARTHENON PRESS, AT NASHVILLE,
TENNESSEE, UNITED STATES OF AMERICA

To our children
Anne, Janice, and Stanley
who live their lives in a world which requires a
Church truly catholic

introduction

A *Church Truly Catholic* will immediately call to the minds of some readers the threefold search of the Consultation on Church Union for a church "truly catholic, truly evangelical, and truly reformed." That is indeed a part of the intended focus of this little volume. It looks beyond that, however, to *catholic* in its root meaning: "according to the whole."

Traditionally *catholic* has connoted historical continuity; its point of reference has been largely toward the past. Often the word projects a narrow and restricted image. Not so, or not necessarily so; for in reality it is all-embracing. Its reference is not only to the past. It includes also the present and is futuristic as well. It has to do with the whole of mankind and with the whole sweep of history and with the whole man. This is the perspective intended here by the designation "a church truly catholic." This is also in

7

accord with the New Testament view of the church. In a word, this usage is the same as that implied by "ecumenical," from *oikoumene*, meaning "the whole inhabited world."

Each of the succeeding chapters or essays is in keeping with this viewpoint. "The Contemporary Context" reviews what, broadly speaking, is going on in the world today. Further, an attempt is made to suggest concurrent developments in the whole church, which is being renewed precisely for more faithful and effective mission in such a world as ours. These developments in the world and in the church are affirmed as the action of God.

The chapter entitled "Methodism and Ecumenism" is not intended to commend in any narrow sense The United Methodist Church. It simply is a statement by one who finds himself in that particular tradition and who, therefore, necessarily speaks from that tradition. The viewpoint is one that approves the fullest participation in and contribution to the ecumenical movement by Methodism. It is unashamed of this "confessional" heritage; for the writer sees confessionalism as legitimate not merely for the sake of confessionalism but for the sake of ecumenism. Each of the great confessional traditions has a rightful and necessary contribution to make to a church truly catholic.

The discussion of "Ministry and Mission" is under this same rubric. The ministry is seen as belonging to the whole church; the present crisis in the ministry is shared by the entire Church. Recovery lies exactly in the whole church being renewed in its

8

service by placing, as it were, new wine in old wine-skins; in rediscovering for our day the classic modes of ministry as they have been shown forth in the experience of Israel and in the life and service of Jesus Christ. In a church truly catholic all the people of God are seen as responsible for commitment to his service. The whole church in each place and in every place should therefore be engaged in the ful-fillment of God's mission. In the fourth chapter, "Worship and the Church's Mission," it is argued that this mission cannot be separated from meaning-ful worship. Recovery in liturgy and recovery in significant mission go hand in hand. The one grows out of and is directed and sustained by the other.

Finally, a church truly catholic is seen as reaching beyond itself. Our concern as Christians today is not merely for the renewal of the church in unity and mission. It looks to the unity of mankind—clearly a New Testament concept, as Ephesians, for example, makes specific. In other words, we move "toward a larger ecumenism." Necessity presses this upon us in a compelling way in a world made small. No easy answers are available for the problem of relationship among the world's great religions. This is a field fraught with difficulties and dangers where one may easily be trapped by false simplicities, or be tempted by least common denominators; where he may suc-cumb to sentimentality on the one hand or im-mobility on the other. Yet we are driven and drawn by the very nature of our faith. Though we can neither predict nor determine the outcome, we can in obedience receive the answers that God him-

9

self may in his good time disclose to us. Here our openness as Christians is called for; our loyalty as Christians is not called into question.

The third chapter was originally given as an address in Baltimore, Maryland, on the occasion of the bicentennial of Methodism in America. The other four chapters constituted the Gray Lectures at Duke University in the fall of 1967. I wish to thank Dean Robert E. Cushman and his colleagues for the courtesies extended to me at the time of their delivery.

In the preparation of such material one incurs debts well beyond the possibility of reckoning, let alone of repaying. By these words of acknowledgment I should like to express appreciation to the multitude of witnesses who have helped me. Beyond that I am thankful for thirty years of deep personal involvement in the missionary and ecumenical movements, first in India and then in the United States. The unusual opportunities afforded me have been incalculably enriching. Finally, I am grateful to God for the gift of life in such a significant era of human history when there are such lively grounds for hope in a church truly catholic.

JAMES K. MATHEWS
BOSTON

contents

Contents

the
contemporary
context

In one of his writings T. S. Eliot affirms that there will always be the church and the world and the heart of man. With these three realities we have to do. They constitute for us the contemporary context.

I begin with the context in which the present-day church finds itself. It is extraordinarily hard to strike fire nowadays, for in the midst of the information explosion everyone has heard everything and felt everything, it seems. A recent definition of poetry speaks of it as making a spark by striking together words of rock and steel. I am not a poet, but let me attempt to strike the steel of the world against the rock of the church, as we must if our hearts are to be reignited with the passion our time requires.

First of all, let us turn to the world. The man of faith acknowledges that God is indeed at work in the world making all things new. This was the theme of the Fourth Assembly of the World Council of Churches at Uppsala. The biblical perspective is that in Christ the old has passed away and the new has come. Long ago this was the song of the prophet Isaiah: "Think not of the far past; dwell not on the deed of old. Here is a new deed of mine springing to light. Have you no eyes to see it?" In our day God is giving us a brand new world. This may seem an obvious and at the same time an imprecise thing to say, but it is a reality that we all experience. We are, in fact, now passing in a striking way from one historical era into another. Matthew Arnold's reference to living between two worlds—one dying and the other powerless to be born—may be more apt for our time than for the time of which he spoke. Or, it may be said that an adult at the beginning of this century would have been more at home in Julius Caesar's world than in our own. This is more like a change in climate than a change in the weather. W. H. Auden suggests the radical quality of this change:

It's as if
    We had left our house for five minutes to
    Mail a letter, and during that time the

14

Living room had changed places with the
Room behind the mirror over the fireplace.[1]

If we have any doubt about the reality of the new
situation, we need only to recall the typical
aversion to modern art and music, symbols of
this strange new world in which we are all actors.
We are unaccustomed to the new backdrop.

God is the author of change, and all the earth-
shaking happenings of our day in some fashion
serve his purpose of expressing through Christ
universal love for the world. I mean the real
world and not an imaginary world conceived as
a kind of ecclesiastical training ground for practice maneuvers by an army of zealous Christians.

A World in Revolution

Some wag has said that only one man in a
million understands the world situation, and it
is astonishing how often you meet him! Though
not a man in a million, I am willing to take the
risk. The most useful, if also the most common,
understanding of our day is that ours has been
a world in revolution. Paul Tillich observed
shortly before his death that we are living in a
historical period of radical and revolutionary
transformation of history. The very word "revo-

[1] "For the Time Being," *Collected Poetry* (New York:
Random House, 1945).

lution" is comparatively new in the sense in which we customarily use it. Until less than three hundred years ago it was a term of astronomy and referred to the heavenly spheres revolving about one another—making music as they did so, as the ancients would have it. Then in the English Revolution, in 1688, the term for the first time came very much down to earth. Now we have had revolutions of volcanic character everywhere. We Americans are likely enough to see "red" whenever we hear the word revolution, except, of course, where it has been sanctified and sanitized in our own history—the American Revolution.

Now, the fact of the matter is that the gospel *is* revolution, if we allow it to be. It offers the possibility of new life for old; it is a yeast that transforms every situation into which it is injected. Of some of the first Christians who allowed the gospel to be what it was, it could be charged: "These men . . . have turned the world upside down" (Acts 17:6 RSV). Here is at least a hint that when the world is turned upside down, the renewing force of the gospel is in some sense at work. We often try to relegate God solely to what we call the "spiritual" realm. Not so, the Bible. It tells of God at work in this world.

1. In our time we have been witnessing a many-faceted revolution of culture that is af-

16

fecting a kind of mutation of civilization. Revolution has clearly been evident in the political realm. There it is rapid, radical, and deep. The balance wheel is off. Expectations rise, and pressures mount. People everywhere want a better nowadays. In 1954 I was in the Congo. The Belgian governor-general of that time said, "Independence? Come back in a hundred years and we'll talk about it!" Independence came with suddenness in 1960, as it has come to more than fifty other nations in recent years. Revolutions never come at convenient times, perhaps because they are on God's timetable and not on man's. Nevertheless, they seem to be prompted by deep-seated and universal human urges—for the better life, for freedom, for equality. We may see these three drives emphasized in turn by the "first" Industrial Revolution of the mid-eighteenth century, the political revolutions of the late eighteenth and nineteenth centuries, and the social revolutions of the mid-nineteenth. The operation of these forces may bring pain and uncertainty. Something of the agonies this can provoke can be seen in these words from a Nigerian poet:

> Here we stand
> infants overblown,
> poised between two civilizations,
> finding the balance irksome

17

itching for something to happen,
to tip us one way or the other
groping in the dark for a helping hand,
and finding none.
I'm tired, O my God,
I'm tired.
I'm tired of standing in the middle way
but where can I go? [2]

Nor is all the excitement restricted to lands afar. Something of its force has been seen in our own country in the Negro revolution. Though this has not always pleased us, at least life is no longer boring. What a time to be alive—when a new deed of God is springing to light, if we but have eyes to see!

2. Of even more immediate importance to us is the scientific revolution that has intruded into every phase of our lives with constantly accelerating force. This development has utterly changed our understanding of ourselves and of our universe and has altered our whole way of thinking. For some the laboratory has become the temple and science the only authority there is. A universe once regarded as fixed is now seen as an expanding one; a straight universe has been replaced by a curved one; a universe long understood as static is now seen as moving according to the laws of relativity. Though modern science is

[2] From "Conflict," copyright by Mabel Imoukhuede.

perhaps three hundred years old, the tempo of its development has increased tremendously during the lifetime of us all. What science has done *for* us is plain to see; what it has done *to* us is still largely hidden from our eyes.

Let us therefore briefly retrace the road mankind has traversed as we have come to this point. It is embarrassing to reflect on the fact that as recently as the century of the discovery of America our Western ancestors still embraced an astonishingly primitive view of the world. Indeed, it had not changed significantly for two thousand years.

Their conception of the universe was, of course, earth-centered. Their world was stationary, with the spheres revolving about the earth. To these several spheres, varying in remoteness of distance from the earth, were attached the moon, the sun, the planets, and the stars. The crystalline spheres themselves were layered in concentric fashion and in model resembled nothing so much as plastic hemispheres protruding from the top of World War II bombers.

Chemistry was then simple. There were only four elementary substances of which all else was composed: fire, air, earth, and water. Likewise simple was the prevailing psychology in which the four humors, corresponding to the four elements, played so important a part. Physics too was elementary. Two principles of motion were

19

known to them: gravity and levity. Earth and water possessed weight, and therefore *gravity* pulled them downward. The "weightless" elements, fire and air, possessed the quality of *levity* and therefore rose up. When they reached a point of equilibrium and purity they constituted the heavenly bodies, which turned in their ethereal spheres as prompted by the moving forces of the divine.

Naturally this view of a multistory world deeply affected man's understanding of himself. His earthly existence could be thought of as an illustration of the principle of *gravity*—he was indeed earthbound. But his aspirations were heavenly; his ideal image was the angelic. He longed for heavenly rest, as it were, for *levity* to replace his *gravity*. His aim and end was for a kind of angelic state of equilibrium, the attainment of a purity that would bring rest and fulfillment, his nature then fully realized.

Such persistent views were subjected to increasing pressures of change, beginning with the seventeenth century or a bit earlier, and were replaced by other outlooks which we have long since come to take for granted. The start of it was with what we usually call the Copernican revolution and came to full fruit with the work of Sir Isaac Newton. Copernicus, almost shyly, became the initiating force in replacing the view of an earth-centered universe for one whose center was the sun. The old idea of invisible but reasonable heavenly spheres, now multiplied in number to conform to new knowledge, had become increasingly untenable. So closely was the old knowledge interrelated in all parts that a drastic overhaul in one part of reality dealt a death blow to the whole medieval structure of learning. A house that had been twenty-five centuries in building finally collapsed.

The capstone of the new arch was laid by Sir Isaac Newton. A new model of the universe was forged. Alexander Pope's lines on Newton come to mind:

> Nature and Nature's laws lay hid in night:
> God said, *Let Newton be!* and all was light.

Naturally a long struggle ensued before such ideas of radical change in world model could be generally accepted. This process was spread over at least two centuries; in fact, in some quarters rudiments of the medieval structure are jealously embraced even in the present day.

These drastic changes were very hard for men to endure, particularly the man of sensitive religious disposition. He was easily bound to traditional views of the universe to such a degree that he could say, "As it was in the beginning, is now and ever shall be." The changes were very painful even to Newton, who somewhat reduced

21

the ache by ejaculating, "O God, I think thy thoughts after thee."

Just how painful the change was can be seen by transposing ourselves for the moment to a quite different culture. Hindu myths, for example, account for an eclipse of the sun by asserting that a dragon is swallowing the sun. Some years ago a teacher friend in India noted that her class was greatly alarmed during the course of a solar eclipse. The students had been prepared for this occurrence by studying the scientific explanation for the phenomenon. The pupils, however, affirmed that the real explanation was the dragon and that if they prayed hard he would not succeed in devouring the heavenly sphere. After a time it became clear that the sun was still intact; they could conclude that their prayers had been answered; hence, their faith in the reality of their world view was powerfully reinforced. Here is a measure of the difficulty that confronts man when his whole universe changes.

As man's ancient view of his world largely determined his view of himself, so Newton's new insights called for similar radical changes in self-understanding. The old world was passive; the new was active. The old was closed; the new was more open. The old was mysterious; the new came to be accounted for by an endless chain of cause and effect. All nature awaited man's ex-

amination and could be made to reveal its se-
crets and its causal network.

Newtonian man had far less heavenly interest
than formerly was the case; he was more earthbound. He was free to examine and to discover.
Yet he himself was bound by the very law of
cause and effect which seemed to liberate him.
Though free, he was captive of forces beyond
himself, whether by external social and economic
forces, as later explained by Marx, or by internal
and psychological forces as elaborated by Freud.
Man has felt himself trapped. This accounts in
large part for the sense of meaninglessness, emp-
tiness, and insignificance that characterizes so
much of our recent literature, written, as it was,
toward the end of Newton's age.

For now Newton's universe has been largely
swept away and replaced by one conceived on
Einstein's model. Again, earth (recently called
the "Spaceship Earth") has shrunken and the
universe has grown. In 1900 the only universe we
knew was that encompassed by the Milky Way.
Now we know that it looks milky because we
view its saucer shape transversely. It is but one
galaxy among 10,000,000,000 others. Once again
the facts no longer fitted into the old picture, so
the picture had to be changed. The idea of
mechanical causation has been replaced by sta-
tistical causation. The law of necessity has been
succeeded by the law of probability. So it is that

23

the modern scientist is more modest and humble than his predecessor of even fifty years ago. The old dogmatic stance of science is now largely gone. Today the scientist knows that he is dealing with a universe which, as it were, is open at both ends.

The tempo of change has quickened. The ancient world view held for twenty-five hundred years; Newton's for about three hundred; and Einstein's is already changing to a post-Einsteinian. The editor of *The Scientific American* says, "There is as much difference between our century and the Nineteenth Century, as there is between the Nineteenth Century and primitive man." How rapidly the transformation has come may be seen by the fact that an adult today has already lived in three worlds. For centuries before us one world served very well for one lifetime. Now we are faced by several.

And with it all man's view of himself has changed. No longer need he feel that his own nature is fixed by prior causes. He is not a victim of circumstances. Rather he enjoys a new freedom. In fact, it may be said that he *is* his freedom. He is not bound by past models; he himself helps forge new models.

We have very sketchily viewed the scientific revolution from the spacious perspectives of physics. It can likewise be seen from the standpoint of biology or mathematics or sociology.

24

The result is, however, much the same regardless of the path one pursues. Here is the point of it for us: The man of faith sees in and through it all the action of God springing into light, if we but have the eyes to see it!

3. Let us now turn to yet another development—the urban revolution. The city is here to stay, and our new world is an urban world. This trend in our time is second in significance only to the intellectual and scientific revolution that I have been describing.

The whole earth may now be regarded as one city. More picturesquely, Marshall McLuhan says the globe is becoming a "tribal village." The reality of this is seen by flying by night up long strips of our east coast, with hardly a break in the lights that reveal human habitation. A similar development is occurring on all the other inhabited continents. The force of this trend is not lost because there are naturally large areas of forests, deserts, and cultivated fields. Yes, the world is one city; or if we could view our globe from a remote satellite it might be seen as six large cities—one for each continent.

Man's first cities were religious ones—shrines in memory of those who had passed into the mystery of death. Priests were the first city planners. Man has not only a religious need, he needs protection; so fortified cities later arose. Men also need the exchange of goods; so finally

25

market cities came into being—economic cities, we would call them. These latter are the cities we have learned to love, for they are living monuments of our history; or these are the cities we have learned to hate for their crowded slums, their inhuman factories, their dinginess, their smog—the things that kill our fellowmen in body and in mind.

But now the possibility of a new kind of city has arisen. It bears the name megalopolis or macropolis. Size, however, is not its determining feature. It is rather the Cultural City, and all that pertains to civilization—to total humanness —belongs to it. The long journey of human settlement has reached a quite new stage. It is this new phenomenon that we must come to understand if we are to understand our day. Half of my life has been lived in large cities, but I must confess to never having profoundly understood the style of life they evoke. Part of this is because of the fact that a certain mystery attaches to urban community; more is because of the fact that our orientation has been directed elsewhere.

At the turn of the century it is estimated that 30 percent of American people were city dwellers and 70 percent lived on the soil or in small towns. Now the figures are almost exactly reversed, and the urban trend is still upward. Suddenly, almost unexpectedly, we have become an urban people in a newly urban world, and even the remotest habitation of man is inescapably affected by this fact. Yet we are almost totally unready for this development, for we as a people almost everywhere have had a rural mind-set. This is more or less acutely felt by this transition generation in which so many of us still have at least one foot in the old rural climate. Our founding fathers conditioned us for this, and no Western man is very far removed from the soil. For Americans, especially, great virtue attaches to tilling the earth. Some of our writers and philosophers have supported this view. Our pictorial myths, whether a Currier and Ives print or a Grandma Moses painting, reinforce our inclination; though even while we gaze at them we know in our heart of hearts that the nostalgia they may stir in us is no longer valid. The rural-urban tension, registered in Congressional redistricting problems or the long resistance to the establishment of a federal Department of Urban Affairs, reflects our persisting rural bias. Our faces are toward megalopolis, but our affections are still down on the farm.

How utterly have our lives changed by our becoming—all of us—an urban people. Notice how great is the contrast between the old and the new! First of all, the rural scene is very large indeed, spacewise. But it opens onto a very small world. The city's external horizons are

27

cramped, but its internal horizons are immense. Second, the rural situation affords a leisurely experience of time—one decision at a time. The urban scene offers a far different experience of time. It brings a sense of haste and presents us with a multitude of possibilities and calls for many decisions. Third, rural life means that persons live more remotely from one another, yet they enjoy great acquaintanceship and mutuality. The city demands close proximity—literally, flesh heaped upon flesh—but remote and highly selective human relations. Fourth, the rural dweller had deep roots in the past. The urban dweller is oriented far more toward the future. As one of our modern poets says, he "remembers the future." Here again we find the measure of our changed world.

Our nostalgia would call us back to a situation that is no longer available to us. Especially our religious instincts attach us sentimentally to some "little brown church in the dale." But there is little reality to all this. It is nonsense to say that "God made the country, but man made the city." No, God is at work in the city too—or even especially at work in the city, inviting the man of today to enter into all culture and make the whole world his home. It is of interest that in Scripture the culmination is reached in a City of God. George Bernard Shaw was not a theologian, but he often expressed astonishing theological insights; as, for instance, when he said, "Beware of the man whose God is in heaven." God is at work among men. In the new city the new deed of God is springing into light, if we but have eyes to see it!

4. We have now hastily scanned the scientific and urban revolutions that have so drastically changed man's life in the world. We have boldly seen in each of these developments the deed of God as Lord of history. This is a way of saying that God loves the world. Yet I need not point out that this is a confession of faith and that the vast majority of humankind see all this solely as the work of man and not at all the work of God. For an intensive new mood characterizes our day—the *secular* mood—and to an astonishing degree it sets the tone of all that happens. In an extreme sense, secularism is life organized as if there were no God. An example of this is the poem that appeared in *Krokodil*, the Russian magazine, soon after their first sputnik was launched:

> And here we have our Sputnik,
> No secret: the newborn planet
> Is modest about its size.
> But this symbol of intellect and light
> Is made by us, and not by the God
> Of the Old Testament.

That is one extreme way of viewing it, but it is as well to remember that in virtually all societies religion today does not have the strong grip upon men that once it did. Bonhoeffer once stated that "almost all of us nowadays conduct our lives for all practical purposes as if God did not exist." Yet in spite of this the Christian faith affirms the action of God in *all* life.

Secularism is idolatrous, but Christianity is the religion of secularization; it moves, as it were, out of the sanctuary and into all life. This is the way the whole world is confronted with Christian history, which alone explains all history. The revolutions we have spoken about have all been carried out in a secular mood, which from our point of view is only a cloak, a camouflage, obscuring from the eyes of those who do not see the deed that God is doing in our midst. The secular is this-worldly, but Christianity also has a this-worldly emphasis. Our task, therefore, is not to accommodate the Rule of God *to* our age—this is a Promethean enterprise—but point out his Lordship *in* our age. The Christian is summoned to beat the secularist at what he thinks is his own game!

What shall be our reaction to this revolution in culture? We can be entirely present to our world as Jesus was. To be, you have to be present. Recall the words from Lincoln's first address to Congress in 1861: "We did not choose the events, . . . the events chose us." We can enter into events as workers together with God. Moreover, we can affirm the world. The bishops at Vatican II did this, for only seventy-five votes were cast against the Pastoral Constitution on the Church in the Modern World. We can see in the political revolution God setting his people free; in the scientific revolution, God asserting his Lordship over the world; in the urban revolution, the coming of a city with foundations that the man of faith has always sought, "whose builder and maker is God." In the secular mood we can see that fulfillment of the hope of the psalmist, "Thou hast given [man] dominion over the works of thy hands," and of Paul when he reminded the earliest Christians, "everything is in your hands."

What is really going on in the world is in some sense the "going-on-ness" of God, who is the Lord of history and who has surprised us by placing us in one of the most exciting periods of all history. Can it be that God is now resting and surveying this new world and declaring that it is "very good"? Revolution may be seen as the turning of an upside-down world upside down so that it is then rightside up. This is not to say that we are to be entirely uncritical of such developments. We need not idolize them. If the world is "God's right hand," then his left hand is his judgment of it. We must be mindful that

31

as man becomes better equipped, he has not by that token become a better man. It is precisely as we stand *in* such a world that we must at the same time stand *over against* it and declare that it is *God's* world. In this very task we are confronted with a strange perplexity: "How shall we sing the Lord's song in a strange land?"

A Church Being Renewed

We have been speaking of the world. Now let us turn to the other pole of our theme. While revolutionary changes have been rocking the world, has the church been static and untouched? Not at all, as the churchman knows so well even though it may be that the outsider is not aware of this. In one of Helmut Thielicke's great sermons he uses the metaphor of the stained-glass windows of a church. From the outside they are dull, colorless, lifeless, devoid of meaning. But on the inside those same windows take on new brilliance, new life, new color and meaning. The man on this inside is becoming aware that we are in one of the most exciting periods of all church history.

Recently I was riding on a plane and found myself seated next to an oceanographer. I asked him what, in particular, oceanographers are excited about these days. He said it was about the Cromwell current—a very swift current or undercurrent, fairly recently discovered in the Pacific. It flows roughly along the Equator from the western Pacific and eastward as far as the Galapagos Islands. Then it is found also in the Atlantic from the east coast of South America and dispersing on the west coast of Africa. It has not yet been discovered in the Indian Ocean.

With a force of a Cromwell current four powerful undercurrents of renewal are sweeping through the life of the whole church today and utterly transforming it.

1. First of all, at the very time of worldwide political revolution, the church is undergoing a renewal with regard to its long-obscured oneness. This development has taken us by surprise. Who would have supposed at the beginning of the present decade that we would have come to a new relationship between the Roman and non-Roman world? Somehow the abyss that once separated us from each other does not seem nearly so wide or so deep as it once did. And across its breadth a word can be heard which is shouted in both directions. It is the word, "Brother!" This is the work of God!

For too long the disunity of the church has been a scandal. It is like Noah's ark: the stench on the inside would not have been endurable if it were not for the storm on the outside. The late Archbishop William Temple once said: 'I believe in One, Holy, Catholic and Apostolic Church and I deeply regret that it does not exist." And yet it does exist. Christians know it does, but the world does not yet know it. Our task in obedience to God is to see that it does. Karl Barth observed long ago that a divided church is "ontologically quite impossible; it is possible only as sin is possible." The time has more than come to renounce our divisiveness as we would renounce sin; that God may heal our divisions.

The goal of full unity may seem a long way from us. Yet in the Apostles' Creed, before we say we believe "in the holy catholic church," we say that we believe "in the Holy Spirit." He can bring it about if we follow his leading. The timing and the manner lie in his initiative.

2. Second, at the very time that a drastic scientific and technological revolution has been going on, the most exciting undercurrent of theological renewal since the Reformation has been taking place. For fifty years this has progressed but has not yet been freely grasped by the church. The great multitude of church members attempt to get a whole lifetime of mileage out of a juvenile view of the Christian faith! John Calvin, in marked contrast, once said that the Christian must all of his life "go to school to Jesus Christ." John Wesley likewise was insistent that

Methodists be an informed people. The same demand is even more upon us today.

The endeavors of contemporary theologians have recovered for the church a sense of the sovereignty of God and his Lordship over all history. Once again, we have been summoned to "let God be God." It is not merely a matter of attempting to grasp him with our minds. Our concrete lives are lived before this sovereign One. He both brings us into being and limits our lives. He says both "Yes" and "No" to us all. Because of this, man has had a new sense of his own creatureliness. To live before God is to live by his grace and to receive all life as a gift. "Wonderful situation," says Pascal, "when the Church depends on God alone."

With the renewal in theology has been a recovery of a sense of the sovereignty of God in the hearts of men, or the acknowledgment of Jesus Christ as Lord. For the intrusion of Christ into history is the most significant fact of all time. Jesus Christ is the humanity of God. In him man receives the one Word by which he can live. To receive this word is to embody it; to take up life and really live in accordance with it.

Then, there has been a recovery of the Holy Spirit, through whom the sovereignty of God is manifested in contemporary life and society; through whom the Word is contemporized. So it is that man has once again received permission to be totally human and engage himself in all seriousness in the civilizing process. Radical obedience is demanded of the Christian who would be engaged in it—an obedience that will result in new structures of justice in the world.

Together with this recovery of the reality of the Triune God has come a fresh understanding of what it means for the church to be the Word-bearing community. The church has more largely recovered its message—which it does not just tell to itself in hopes that the world will overhear, but offers in direct address to the world —God's permission to all people to live their lives as men before him.

3. Third, at precisely the time of urban revolution the church is experiencing a renewal in respect to its *liturgy*. Starting with the Roman Catholics, partly on lay initiative, this movement has spread far beyond Roman borders. Most free churchmen tend to be suspicious of liturgy. It is often understood as a kind of "high church" emphasis. Actually it is just the opposite and aims at bringing the laity more fully into public worship, so making it what in reality it is, "the work of the people of God." Yet how terrified is the average layman when the pastor calls on him to pray. Liturgy is therefore fundamental for the Christian. If one wonders what relation this may have to the urban revolution, it is as well to

recall that the word "liturgist" in Greek means "director of public works." This suggests that worship is immensely relevant to everyday living. It is never a mere aesthetic experience. In Roman Catholic circles today it is increasingly understood that Mass is not something said, but something done in obedience to the Lord who said: "Do this." It is our reminder that we are to act in the world after the manner of Christ. Worship is renewal of our true being. We cannot be genuine Christians except as we return again and again to the "cobalt pile of prayer."

We worship God and address him as Father, for he addresses us as his children. We worship "through Jesus Christ our Lord," for through Jesus Christ, God has given himself to the world and we give ourselves to God. We worship God in the Holy Spirit, through whom the Word becomes contemporary. So we worship "in the name of the Father and of the Son and of the Holy Spirit." We appear before God not just in our own right but in behalf of all mankind. There is a continuity between our worship and everything else we do. The Reformers saw that "the whole duty of man was to glorify God and enjoy him forever."

This is to suggest a twofold aspect to worship. It is first of all an exaltation of God. It is, secondly, an understanding of the meaning of our own lives. The service of worship may be seen as a drama, but not a spectator drama. All present are actors. The minister of worship is not cast in the leading role; rather, he is the prompter. There are no stellar roles. Even more it may be understood as rehearsal for the real drama, which takes place outside the sanctuary in everyday life. In worship the Christian rediscovers his true identity so that in everyday-ness he can exercise his proper responsibility. Worship is something Christians *do* with their whole beings. There is, in fact, a kind of choreography about it; a gathering together to celebrate and a scattering in the world to serve.

The service of worship is, therefore, only a prelude to service in the world. But before we go out the benediction is said. It is not in reality a prayer. Rather it is a final word of reassurance of one Christian to others. It should be said with pastor and people looking in one another's eyes. "The grace of our Lord Jesus Christ, which is the love of God the Father, made real and present by the Holy Spirit, is yours now and always." Then the people, not the pastor, say "Amen." That is their way of returning to him the reassurance that all the resources of God for daily living are freely given to his people. Then they go out to live. This is what happens every time we engage in corporate worship. It is particularly dramatic in the Eucharist—the service of Holy Communion. "Do this in remembrance of me"

38

is in the plural. No Christian lives unto himself. There is also continuity about it, for not a day has passed since Pentecost in which Christians have not met together to celebrate the death and resurrection of Jesus Christ.

4. Fourth, at the very time of what may be called the secular revolution, the church in our time is undergoing renewal with respect to the *laity*. During World War II in Europe it became clear that the church as it was conventionally understood was not sufficient to the situation. The merely worshiping community could be too easily controlled and restrained by totalitarian regimes. It was seen afresh that the church is wherever the Christian is. The church is not just where the gospel is preached and the sacraments administered. It is also, or rather, wherever the gospel is lived.

This amounted to a recovery of an insight taken for granted in the early church. Someone has put it very sharply in the following way: "If you had arrived in Corinth at ten o'clock on a Friday morning when Paul was there and had asked, as one would today, for 'the church,' you might have found someone who understood what you were looking for. When you did find a member and asked him, 'Where is the church?' he might have replied, 'Well, I'm here; Paul is probably making tents; others are at whatever work they do. We meet for worship on Sunday in Stephana's house.' "

The "laity" refers to the whole people of God. And every one of them has a ministry. For this they are ordained at baptism. The weight of being free men has driven them back for renewal. The congregation helps laymen "live their baptism." The ministry of the laity is not opposed to that of the ordained pastor. Rather they complement each other. Their ministry is actually one; they mutually sustain each other. The ordained ministry functions, in the main, within the church; the layman ministers in the world at his daily task, to manifest Jesus Christ there. Of this we shall have more to say later.

Now, all four of these movements of renewal are going on today without regard for denomination or tradition. The very simultaneity and universality of them is evidence for the man of faith, of their being the work of God in our midst. It has been given to us of this generation to live in one of the great periods of the church, when God is so evidently intending its renewal. God wills a brand new church for a brand new world! By ecumenical renewal we mean recovery of the church's given oneness; by theological renewal, let God be God; by liturgical renewal, inviting the people once again to live their lives in the praise of God; by renewal of the laity, restoring to them their share in the ministry of Christ. If

40

one would be involved in church renewal, let him seize upon one of these four and he will be led to involvement in the other three.

We have viewed the world as shaken by a profound revolution in culture that may be rich in promise, and the church swept profoundly by powerful undercurrents of renewal, full of hope. What of the heart of man? Is he not often torn by deep inward problems, greatly intensified by the bewildering changes in which he is often caught and which shape his life from the outside? Is he not threatened with loss of freedom, loss of a sense of the holy, tempted by new forms of idolatry? Can the church bring the Living Word to man in such a setting; awaken in him the sense of the holy; call him to judgment and "new mindedness" (*metanoia*); and offer him God's gift of acceptance and significance in the name of Jesus Christ? If so, then "shivering and fluttering" though he may be—as the poet has it—he may know himself chosen and free to choose his destiny.

united
methodism
and ecumenism

The previous chapter spoke of the contemporary context in which we are called upon to live and to serve. We find ourselves in a strange new world. We affirmed that God is at work in the great movements of our time, that these are ways that God loves the world; so must we if we are to be fellow workers with him. Likewise, in mighty movements he is renewing his church. One may well join with the octogenarian—blind, crippled, bedridden for years—who exclaimed not long ago: "What a time to be alive, when God is so evidently at work in his church!"

We turn now to "United Methodism and Ecumenism." The two belong together, and both suffer if they are separated. Ecumenism is a rightful part of our heritage. Though surely not the last word, nevertheless an important word on this subject was voiced by John Wesley in his great sermon on the "Catholic Spirit." He places this theme in the context of the debt of love that is "due to all mankind." He pleads for a "union in affection" while awaiting what he calls "entire external union." He then describes the man of catholic spirit:

. . . His heart is enlarged toward all mankind, those he knows and those he does not; he embraces with strong and cordial affection, neighbours and strangers, friends and enemies. This is catholic or universal love. And he that has this is of a catholic spirit. For love alone gives the title to this character: Catholic love is a catholic spirit.

We have scarcely come up to that, let alone surpassed it. Similarly, the early leaders of both the Evangelical and United Brethren traditions were cooperative and well disposed toward Christian unity. United Methodism has rightful cause to "get right" with ecumenism.

By ecumenism, we do not refer solely, and perhaps not even primarily, to the coming together of the churches. It has more to do with the relation of the church to the world than of the church to church. Its basic perspective is "the whole inhabited world," which the word ecumenism means literally. It has to do with a profound stirring in the depths of men—of all men—and a shaking of their orders to the foundation. It embraces also the whole sweep of history. Its reference is to what God intends among men, "namely, that the universe . . . might be brought into a unity in Christ," as Ephesians has it.

Moreover, in this generation we are able to experience ourselves in a new way, a comprehensive way. By this I mean that we now know ourselves to be global persons. We are no longer confined to national or racial boundaries. Whatever concerns any man anywhere concerns us. This means that all provincialism and all parochialism must be put aside. Our interest is now humanity itself, and we may comprehend the whole *oikoumene*.

In a more specific sense ecumenism connotes the whole church throughout the whole inhabited world, particularly as it reaches toward a fuller and more visible expression of its unity. I have referred to the expression attributed to Archbishop William Temple that he believed in One, Holy, Catholic and Apostolic Church—and regretted very much that it did not exist. This must have been voiced in a discouraging moment, for he was himself one of the great architects of the ecumenical movement and called it, in his oft-quoted enthronement sermon at York, "the great new fact of our time." More than that, in his letter of invitation written in 1937 to the churches looking toward the establishment of the World Council of Churches he said, "We are obliged to express the amount of unity we can express at this time." That is considerable, and the whole of it may be viewed as the present expression of churchly ecumenism. It should not be forgotten that the church's greatest contribution to the contemporary world —politically speaking—is this very fact of its worldwide-ness.

It hardly need be stated that the ecumenical movement has an essentially missionary origin. It is as if missionaries sent out by their various traditions found themselves at the same task, along the same road, in obedience to the same Lord. It is as if they said: "Why not *walk* together?" and they did. Sooner or later this raised the further question: "Why not *be* together?"

Nowadays we all have many irons in the ecumenical fire. One of them is *cooperation* in a conciliar fashion, whether locally or on a state, national, or world level. None of these is perfect, but if, for example, the National Christian Council were to be abolished today, another one would have to be organized tomorrow.

Once again, 235 churches in 80 countries cooperate through the World Council of Churches. The basis of the Council makes clear the nature of this working together: "The

World Council of Churches is a fellowship of churches which confess the Lord Jesus Christ as God and Savior, according to the Scriptures and seek to fulfill together their common calling to the glory of the one God, Father, Son and Holy Spirit." It should be clear that the World Council of Churches is *not* the ecumenical movement but one of its many manifestations and chief vehicles. It should be noted that all but one of the autocephalous churches of Orthodoxy are now members; so they are more *in* the World Council than the rest of us are. The growing experience of interrelation between Rome and Geneva is also of the utmost importance. The World Council faithfully endeavors to carry on the work instituted and formerly carried on by the International Missionary Council (John R. Mott); the Faith and Order Movement (Bishop C. H. Brent); and the Life and Work Movement (Archbishop Nathan Söderblom).

A bit of serendipity is involved in membership in the World Council. It tends to put our denominations in proper perspective. We may seem unduly important because of our size in given nations: Methodists in the United States, Anglicans in Britain, Lutherans in Germany. Though we may join the Council out of cooperative interest, all of us experience in it a fuller catholicity and together give fuller expression to the universality that the gospel both authorizes and demands.

United Methodists carry their full share of the load in the cooperative movement. We are also related with a score of other Wesleyan branches in the World Methodist Council. The seven worldwide confessional groups (though Methodism is not, strictly speaking, confessional) constitute a special dimension of ecumenism. At one time these groups were called into question by the "true believers" of the ecumenical movement and accused of "militant scholastic devotion to schism." Not so, nowadays. It was through world confessional bodies, for example, that observers were chosen for Vatican II—an almost impossible undertaking otherwise. While the dangers of "spiritual narcissism" must be acknowledged, it is now seen more clearly that there is a positive role for the confessional bodies at this stage of the ecumenical journey. They need not be regarded, nor need regard they themselves, as ecclesiastical power blocs, nor defenders of a kind of churchly tribalism. They may serve the church universal by being confessional not for the sake of confessionalism, but for the sake of ecumenism. During recent years the World Methodist Council has taken steps to revise its structure and program more fully to serve this higher end.

47

Meanwhile The United Methodist Church is engaging in prolonged studies of the best ways for its Central Conferences outside the United States to relate to the General Conference. I shall not endeavor to discuss this in detail. Does the future lie in continued development of what has emerged from the past? Or shall each part become autonomous? Or shall a new type of World Methodist Church emerge? My own views on this matter may seem conservative. For those parts of The United Methodist Church which lie in other lands than the United States, autonomy ought always to be available and that without any question. As to a new type of World Methodist Church, I am skeptical. This is very late in the ecumenical day and would consume enormous amounts of energy with little resultant benefits. Rather, I would prefer to stay with our present structure which is clearly in a state of dynamic flux. We should immediately arrange for practical autonomy in association with the General Conference. And we should work rapidly toward church union in all areas, maintaining some form of international ecclesiastical structure to bequeath, if possible, to these unions.

This brings us to church union as one of the possible fruits of ecumenism. About this in its more comprehensive form of COCU (Consultation on Church Union) I shall turn later in this chapter. At the present time twenty-seven union schemes are under discussion in twenty-six different countries. Major plans are afoot in Australia, Canada, Nigeria, Kenya, Tanzania, and in the United Kingdom. The recent past has not augured well for union in any of these places for a variety of reasons. In the United States we have done better, for the Evangelical United Brethren (E.U.B.)–Methodist union has taken place. I share the feelings of those who wish that the form of union could have been more exciting and renewing, rather than smacking so much as it did of a business merger. Nevertheless, in this case, as in so many others, possibly the excitement will come after marriage rather than before. Meanwhile all concerned ought to bend their efforts to see to it that bold risks of faith are taken to make The United Methodist Church an obedient servant of our Lord. In any event, our ecumenical responsibility for the twentieth century will not have been discharged by this move alone.[1]

We have spoken of conciliar cooperation, confessionalism, and church union. There is also that form of ecumenism which is expressed in *conversation*—dialogue—and this is taking

[1] The Uniting Conference in Dallas exceeded everyone's expectations and was a kind of Methodist "Vatican II." It will be remembered as one of the great church assemblies of the century.

49

place on every hand. As is well known, the World Council of Churches has a Joint Working Group with the Roman Catholic Church. There are also dialogue groups between the Vatican and several of the world confessional bodies, including the World Methodist Council. Similarly such interchanges are taking place between the Orthodox and other traditions ("dialogue of love"); or between confessional groups; or between member churches within the various denominational families, such as British-American Methodists. In the United States at present dialogue is proceeding on various subjects between the Roman Catholics and the Orthodox (theological, pastoral, practical matters); Reformed (theology, worship, and mission); Lutherans (Eucharist and doctrine), Episcopalians (ministry and Eucharist); Methodists, Disciples, and Baptists (baptism).

Nor should we overlook the quieter, less formal but no less important conversations going on periodically between the classical Protestant groups and the conservative evangelicals. An even more striking development is the increasing discussion between Christians and Marxists. At a recent meeting in Czechoslovakia they found common ground in the responsibility for the future of man and search for the meaning of human existence. Finally, an important step in making ecumenism a people's movement has been taken through "Living Room Dialogues," for which two guidebooks have been published. Why dialogue? One reason for it is better mutual understanding, of course, but another was voiced at Lund in 1952: "There are truths about the nature of God and His Church which will remain forever closed to us unless we act together in obedience to the unity which is already ours." Moreover, we are discovering how very much alike we are. Gordon Rupp once told a Roman Catholic friend: "Very roughly, I mean by 'Protestant' what you mean by 'Catholic.'"

A few words about the progress of Roman Catholic–United Methodist discussion are in order. So far we have had four sessions in an atmosphere of seriousness, yet openness and congeniality. At the first session the groundwork was laid; at the second, papers were prepared from both sides on the nature of faith and the relation of faith and good works. The third session dealt with the doctrine of the Holy Spirit in the two churches. A fourth meeting at Fordham University dealt with the more sensitive practical problem of parochial schools. The quality of papers has been high, and large areas of basic agreement have been found. Publication of the documents and wider involvement of our constituencies in the discussion of issues are great needs at present.

51

We have already come to speak of this matter of dialogue as if it were commonplace, rather than what it really is: the result of the most unexpected and revolutionary transformation of attitude on the part of Rome. And it has happened before our unbelieving eyes in this very decade. In other words, Protestant churches no longer are seen by our Roman Catholic brethren as existing contrary to the will of God, but are understood precisely to be churches. Therefore, significant dialogue *can* take place between *churches* and not just individual Christians. In other words, it is possible to hold "discussions of theological problems, where each can deal with the other on equal footing," as the Decree on Ecumenism specifically states. This development is of the most profound importance for the future of joint enterprise in faith and action in the contemporary world.

For a thaw in the icy relations between the Roman Catholic Church and the rest of us is a reality. It is impossible to keep up with its developments: a formal message from the Council of Bishops of The Methodist Church to the Fathers of Vatican Council II and reply by Cardinal Bea; agreement on a common Hebrew and Greek text for the Bible and projects for joint translations in some forty languages; the mutual repudiation of ancient anathemas by the Sees of both Rome and Constantinople;

papal approval of the Revised Standard Version for use in English Masses; the shift in emphasis from the first word to the second in the designation, "separated brethren"; ecumenical services in countless communities; the appointment of a Jesuit, Fr. David J. Bowman, to the staff of the National Council of Churches. To all this may we not very humbly give witness that "this is the Lord's doing, and marvelous in our eyes"?

All this results from the Roman Catholics joining in the ecumenical movement (as recently as 1954 they specifically frowned on it), "Johnny-Come-Latelys" by their own admission. And all this as a result of the boldness of a lively little old man who was to be merely an "interim pope," John XXIII, who dared to open the windows of the Church of Rome that the refreshing breezes of God might blow through. The result has been what may have been termed a Roman Catholic Reformation. Karl Barth allowed that in this respect they may well have outpaced contemporary Protestantism. It is Rome that has become the chief vehicle of renewal in the contemporary church.

It is not my purpose to discuss Vatican II in detail. Much has already been heard and written about it from competent observers. But we cannot responsibly fail to turn attention to this matter, for no man anywhere can nowadays live as if Vatican II had never happened.

It was my privilege to be a special visitor in Rome during a period of the fourth and final session of the Council. Though not an official observer, I received the same courtesies that were afforded that group. Observers had also been invited to Trent and, condescendingly, to Vatican I. We have recently celebrated the 450th anniversary of Martin Luther's having nailed the 95 theses to the church door in Wittenberg, and it would not be inappropriate to mention that while I was there the very delicate question of indulgences was discussed. This was not officially one of the *schemata,* and I recall the acute embarrassment that prevailed during this discussion. It was reflected accurately to me by the young American priest who was assigned to me as interpreter. One of the bishops was frank enough to acknowledge on the floor of St. Peter's that this was the focal issue that had triggered the Reformation and that the very basilica in which they were meeting had been built largely from the sale of indulgences. Luther, it will be recalled, did not object to them as such but to the extreme abuses that attended their dispensing, particularly by the Dominican monk Tetzel.

No action was taken by the Council, but elaborate measures were taken to explain this subject to the press and visitors. Monsignor Gregory Baum acknowledged that indulgences symbolized all that Protestants feel about Rome. He himself complained about the system being considered a kind of dispensation from a "treasury of merits" of ecclesiastical "counterpart funds." He then demythologized the term in a manner that might be acceptable to the most stouthearted Protestant. "Indulgences," he said, "were special forms of prayers of the Church, relying on the presence of Christ in her midst and hence confident that the prayer would be heard, beseeching God to draw toward complete reconciliation this or that pardoned sinner who is in special need of it." In other words, responsible intercession by the whole church for its wayward members is what indulgences mean.

For some parts of the Roman Church indulgences would seem to be a lively contemporary issue, but not for most parts. In other words, it is precisely an illustration of why Vatican II was necessary. As Cardinal Cushing once told me: "We simply *had* to have the Council." Its aim was *aggiornamento*—updating of the Church in the face of the modern world. Indeed, the whole work of the Council may be seen as moving within the polarity of the Church and the modern world. Naturally this step was full of deep risks and perils—of oversecularization, of apostasy, of schism—but these were dangers that had to be accepted. So the theological reflection upon the pastoral and apostolic (evangelistic)

55

life of the church, which in essence was the task of the Council, was launched and carried through. Vatican II has already become one of the great symbols of the twentieth century. When John XXIII announced it, it was a kind of breaking loose in the spirit of man, a breaking through of God, the possibility of a Christian people to become in reality the "people of God."

The physical setting, the procedures, the spiritual atmosphere were all impressive and unforgettable. Those who were present at all sessions have tried to characterize them and suggest their mood:

CHARACTER	MOOD
Session IV. Conciliation	Expectant Excitement
Session I. Presentation	Tension and Gloom
Session II. Contest	Sobriety
Session III. Victory	Irenic, joyful, hope

An incredible amount of business was done. Hundreds of schemata were proposed; then reduced to twenty-five; then to sixteen. Thousands of *modi* were considered, as were the many suggestions of the observers. Votes steadily moved in the direction of unanimity on the various schemata. The yield was immense: four constitutions, nine decrees, and three declarations—enough to keep post-conciliar commissions, canon lawyers, and scholars well occupied for a generation to come.

Interestingly enough, not all suggestions offered by either Pope were accepted. They seldom intervened but conducted themselves with an informed detachment much different from that which obtained in Vatican I. The contrasts of John and Paul are significant. The former simple but not naïve; a determined innovator. The latter sophisticated yet kindly; a skillful, meticulous, conciliatory administrator. It took John to start a council but Paul to carry one through to completion.

In sum, Vatican II was a modern miracle— the impossible had happened, the immobile had moved. It was a venture in international adult education *par excellence*. Just imagine what it has meant for twenty-five hundred of the top leaders of a great institution to go aside for fourteen weeks, four years in a row, to come to know one another and to sit at the feet of the greatest minds that institution affords. Just suppose some counterpart step might be taken, for example, by the bishops of The United Methodist Church! Renewal would be well on the way! In Rome a new morale was released; a new momentum generated. A new openness characterizes the Roman Church, and a new opportunity confronts her.

More than this, the Roman Church has become obedient to the Protestant principle. By this I do not mean that she has become a Protestant church, as some of her own traditionalists fear. I take the Protestant principle, quite simply, to mean that all institutions among men are under the sovereign judgment of God and subject to renewal by the Holy Spirit. Let it be said further, that while this has been happening in Rome, a kind of glorious content in the status quo has overtaken much of Protestantism. Much in our churches is pre-Reformation.

So a curious turn of the tables of history has taken place: where we thought we sat, there sits Rome today, and in the place we had assigned to Roman Catholics, behold, we Protestants are largely sitting there today! There is, therefore, no room for pretense on our part, and we might very well consider how much we have espoused that Rome has now abandoned. Meanwhile we may equally well rejoice at this powerful reinforcement of the ecumenical movement and the fuller thrust toward Christian unity. I repeat the irony: though in some sense Luther and the Reformation have won, we heirs of Luther are in no position to gloat over the fact and are deprived of that very experience of triumphalism which we might most earnestly have desired.

Our attention needs to be on not merely what the Council achieved, but what was made possible. The greatest achievement of Vatican II is threefold: ecclesiological development, liturgical reform, and incarnational mission to the modern world.

The first development is set forth principally in The Dogmatic Constitution on the Church, called the *Lumen Gentium*. This is far and away the most important Vatican II document, and is historic from the standpoint that it is, surprisingly, the first time the doctrine of the church has had formal conciliar definition. It breaks new ground in its emphasis on the church as the people of God, a more biblical and eschatological motif. Here, too, the non-Roman bodies are seen as churches, and the whole outlook is more soundly ecumenical. Moreover, here is set forth the concept of collegiality regarded by many as *the* most important development of Vatican II. By extension, collegiality is seen as embracing not only the Bishop of Rome and other bishops but derivatively all clergy and laity; indeed, all the people of God. In this context, a certain semi-autonomous position is afforded national churches within Roman Catholicism—all in communion with the Bishop of Rome. Here, too, is set forth the role of the Blessed Virgin Mary, described in a way that somewhat minimizes the teaching vis-à-vis more extreme Marian tendencies in Rome.

59

Regarding liturgy (The Constitution on the Sacred Liturgy) the laity are more directly affected and their fuller participation made possible. The liturgy has been made more open and a fuller place afforded for the Bible in the life of the Church. It is sometimes said by Protestants today: "The trouble with you Catholics is that you're always quoting Scripture!" The liturgy has been made simpler and more intelligible. Now authority has been given in the United States for Anglicizing the whole Mass, including the Canon. Thus another of our Articles of Religion concerning our attitude toward the Roman Church becomes inoperative. Though such developments are upsetting and even traumatic to the aged and the conservative, on the whole liturgical reform is being well received by Roman Catholics.

The third emphasis, on mission to the modern world, is set forth in a pastoral constitution and affords a perspective that encourages far more effective witness and service on the contemporary scene.

If the achievements are impressive, the problems and continuing responsibilities are well nigh overwhelming. These involve the implementation of the Council both within and outside the Church. This is a prime task of the Synod of Bishops, which has just met in Rome. In other words, the Council itself was only a beginning. Within the life of the Church we may expect a period ahead of turbulence, involving some disillusionment and disenchantment, some crisis in faith, some falling away. For the teaching authority of the Church has been shaken, and it will take time to reestablish psychological stability amongst both clergy and laity. With regard to ecumenical relations there will be some apathy; premature satisfaction with the distance already covered; a possible flight from concern about unity of the churches to that secular ecumenism which concerns itself mostly about the task in the world. We Protestants have real responsibilities to discharge ourselves in all these respects.

What then are we to say? All our problems of difference are not by any means resolved. Practical matters, such as mixed marriages, trouble us deeply as, of course, do the views of the papacy and Mariology. Much accommodation has been made on Rome's side, but who says she must do all the accommodating? Significantly, the issues dividing us now are not the same issues that obtained in Luther's day. In large measure the ball has been thrown back into our side of the court.

The future is in God's hands. Meanwhile we can get to know one another better, we can respect one another. We can repudiate our repudiations. We can and must pray for one

61

another. We can hold one another responsible for the highest insights God has given us and the highest profession we make. We can reaffirm our vast common heritage. Berdyaev used to say that the trouble with Roman Catholics and Protestants was that he, as an Orthodox Christian, could not tell them apart. We can do vastly more together and learn what ecumenism is by *doing* it, and so move together, as Abbé Couturier once put it, toward "unity at the time God sets and with the means He gives."

Douglas Horton shares this moving story told by Pope Paul VI at the last meeting with the observers at Rome:

We were told, many years ago, about a charming and symbolic episode from the life of one of the great Eastern Church thinkers of modern times, and we tell it to you as we remember it. It seems to us it was about Soloviev. At one time, while staying in a monastery, he had been having a spiritual conversation until a late hour with a pious monk. Finally, wishing to return to his cell, he went out into the corridor on which opened the doors of the cells, all alike and all equally closed. In the dark he was not able to identify the door of the cell which had been assigned to him. On the other hand, he felt it impossible to return to the cell of the monk he had just left and he did not want to disturb anyone else during the rigorous monastic silence of the night. Thus the philosopher resigned himself to pass the night walking slowly up and down the monastery corridor, suddenly become mysterious and inhospitable, absorbed in his thoughts. The night was long and dreary but at last it passed and with the first light of dawn the tired philosopher easily recognized the door to his cell which he had passed time and time again during the night. And he remarked: It is often thus with those who search for truth. They pass right by it during their wakefulness without seeing it until a ray of the sunlight of divine wisdom makes so easy and happy the consoling revelation." [2]

Or hear these words of John Wesley in his famous letter to a Roman Catholic:

In the name, then, and in the strength of God, let us resolve, first, not to hurt one another. . . . Let us resolve, secondly, God being our helper, to speak nothing harsh or unkind of each other. The sure way to avoid this is to say all the good we can both of and to one another. . . . Let us, thirdly, resolve to harbour no unkind thought, no unfriendly temper towards each other. . . . Let us, fourthly endeavor to help each other. . . .

O let you and I (whatever others do) press on to the prize of our high calling! that, being justified by faith, we may have peace with God through our Lord Jesus Christ; that we may rejoice in God through Jesus Christ, by whom we have received the atonement; that the love of God may be shed

[2] Douglas Horton, *Toward an Undivided Church* (New York: Association Press, 1967), pp. 61-62.

abroad in our hearts by the Holy Ghost which is given unto us. Let us count all things but loss for the excellency of the knowledge of Jesus Christ our Lord; being ready for Him to suffer the loss of all things, and counting them but dung, that we may win Christ.

We turn our attention now to another phase of ecumenism. Not long ago a thoughtful lay-woman said in my presence that two events in the church in our time had given her an exhil-arating sense of liberation. One of these was Vatican II, to which we have just been giving some attention. The other was the Consultation on Church Union. Let us now consider it brief-ly. If, in the first case, the impossible has hap-pened, in the other the improbable has at least become possible. Indeed, COCU confronts us with the most creative possibility in American Protestantism today.

It is surely a significant fact that ten denom-inations in the United States are embarked to-gether on voyage of exploration and discovery of a church united which is "truly catholic, truly evangelical, truly reformed." By "truly catholic" we mean quite literally "according to the whole," emphasizing and embracing the Chris-tian faith in its wholeness, its inclusiveness, its continuity. By "truly evangelical" we mean the joyful response to, adherence to, and obedience

64

to the whole gospel in faith and practice and commending it to all men. By "truly reformed" we mean the continuous submission of ourselves and the institutional church to the judgment of God and renewal by the Holy Spirit.

Father Ives Congar likens the church to water in a lake. Whence comes the water? From the evangelical standpoint it comes down vertically as rain; from the catholic viewpoint it comes horizontally by rivers and canals. We might extend his metaphor and say that from the reformed point of view God controls both the rain and the floodgates.

COCU is a lively manifestation of the ecumenical movement and is very much a part of the twentieth-century struggle toward a more visible unity of the church. For several centuries the story has been one of divisions. This has been taken for granted in the United States. We brought our churches along with us; we have started our own; we have segregated ourselves in them by language and color; we have reflected in them our sociological differences, and more often than not we have gloried in this process. If there is virtue in variety, we are of all people most virtuous. We have claimed that there was power generated by our separateness; but has it always been of the Lord, or have we been consumed by zeal for our own houses? Or may we not observe that power is indeed generated by nuclear fission—the splitting of the atom—but far greater power is produced by nuclear fusion —the uniting of atoms?

But now in our sorely divided world, the world itself seems to be saying to the church: "Physician, heal thyself!" Is there anything clearer than that God is leading his people into fuller unity? As Archbishop Nathan Söderblom declared long ago, "God wills it and the world's need requires it." Or at the Faith and Order Conference in Lund, 1952, this insight was given: "We are agreed that there are not two churches, one visible and one invisible, but one Church which must find visible expression on earth." This is the stream in which COCU finds itself.

Not only are we in a common setting, but we are faced by common demands. What I have in mind is what Dr. W. A. Visser 't Hooft writes about in *The Pressures of Our Common Calling*. We are not merely prompted by fears— therefore, let us group together against the impending storm as we pass through the fearful wilderness ahead. The cynic observes that no doubt the Gadarene swine said as they headed for the precipice: "We must keep moving and stay together." We are not prompted only by the insight of Bishop Brent: "The world is too strong for a divided church." Nor are we urged on by the fact that the human mind finally resists contradictions and seeks the most unifying concepts. We do not take our cue from the wisdom of the marketplace and seek to "merge" for reasons of efficiency and economy. And we are not spurred on by the kind of exasperation that led a German Lutheran pastor to say at New Delhi, "I can no longer stand a divided Lord's table!" But, quite simply, we are prompted by the fact that the church *is* one. This is the point of departure. The New Testament knows but one church, though it manifested variety and undoubted tension. When Paul asks the patently absurd question of the Corinthians, "Is Christ divided?" he meant it to be answered by a resounding "No." Then he goes on powerfully to affirm the church's oneness. An insight insisted upon in the ecumenical movement at an early stage was that the word "church" had no plural.

When he was a student in this country Dietrich Bonhoeffer wrote: "The unity of the church of Jesus Christ is to American Christianity less something essential, originally given by God, than something required, something which ought to be. It is less origin than goal." [3] He felt that in Europe the opposite view was more true. Just suppose that we should deliberately reverse this situation, that we should

[3] *No Rusty Swords*, ed. Edwin H. Robertson (New York: Harper & Row, 1965), p. 97.

67

take *given unity* as our starting point; then our search would be for giving this fuller manifestation.

The church *is* one. Therefore, its continued divided state is disobedience to God—it contradicts its own nature; it distorts its witness; it frustrates its mission. Just turn for a moment to the Republic of South Africa, where the government's basic policy is *apartheid*, which literally means "separation." Here would appear to be a wonderful place to demonstrate the church's oneness. But what do we find there? The church is more sorely divided than in any other part of the world, with some 1,500 different denominations among a population of possibly 12,000,000! No wonder the sundered Body of Christ is called his "sixth wound"!

We may therefore rejoice in every evidence of progress toward the fuller unity God intends. Consider this familiar statement:

We believe that the unity which is both God's will and his gift to his Church is being made visible as all in each place who are baptized into Jesus Christ and confess him as Lord and Saviour are brought by the Holy Spirit into ONE fully committed fellowship, holding the one apostolic faith, preaching the one Gospel, breaking the one bread, joining in common prayer, and having a corporate life reaching out in witness and service to all and who at the same time are united with the whole

Christian fellowship in all places and in all ages in such wise that ministry and members are accepted by all, and that all can act and speak together as occasion requires for the tasks to which God calls his people.[4]

Surely this lengthy description is the greatest single sentence yet to come out of the ecumenical movement!

I assume a general acquaintance with the Consultation:[5] that it was in one sense inaugurated in response to the sermon preached by Dr. Eugene Carson Blake at Grace Episcopal Cathedral in San Francisco on December 4, 1960—though behind it lay many previous efforts and conversations, and, we trust, the guidance of God; that ten denominations representing some twenty-eight million members are now participants; that a number of other churches have an observer-consultant relationship to it; that annual sessions have explored backgrounds, possibilities, and difficulties from many angles; that an increasing volume of documents concerning it have accumulated; that a partial outline of a plan of union has emerged; that interest and commitment of the member churches continues

[4] *New Delhi Speaks*, a report from the World Council of Churches Third Assembly, ed. W. A. Visser 't Hooft, (New York: Association Press, 1962), pp. 92-93.
[5] See *Principles of Church Union*, Reports of the Four COCU Meetings (Cincinnati, Forward Movement, 1967).

69

unabated; that a draft Plan of Union is scheduled for March, 1970.

Thus far the process has been one of sharing gifts. In doing so each denomination has discovered new things about itself, for no tradition has mined all its treasures. Moreover, we are beginning to comprehend the meaning of the gifts others have to bring; for example, the remarkable heritage of continuity in worship and ministry of the Episcopalians; the United Church of Christ and Disciples' emphasis on congregational order and freedom; the Presbyterian sense of confessional integrity and corporate order. And what of United Methodists? Perhaps their most useful contribution is emphasis on connectional polity and their insight that matters of both Faith and Order are instrumental to nurture and mission. No church can say to others, "We have no need of you." Along the way we have discovered we are not as different from one another as we might have supposed. Archbishop Geoffrey Fisher said at Amsterdam, "We may not like each other but we are strangely alike." There is undoubtedly a greater range of difference within our denominations than between them. Always a brotherly spirit has prevailed in the Consultation.

So far we have found remarkable areas of agreement on many things, and these are reflected in the *Principles of Church Union*, chapter by chapter. For instance, we do not differ much on essentials of faith, only in accent. For in our day the whole church has been *given* what may well be called an ecumenical faith. Nor do we vary widely in matters of worship and sacrament. On ministry we are farther apart— especially in practice and emphasis—but in principle the participants seem prepared to acknowledge three offices of ordained ministry: the diaconate, the presbyterate, and the episcopate—the latter to be historic and constitutionally defined. Now all of these bristle with questions that must be pressed hard and long. These should be asked, but the old inflexibility that once related to them is no longer as pronounced as was once the case. Oddly enough, it is structure that excites the most defensiveness, for no one wishes to move into unaccustomed surroundings. At the recent COCU session in Cambridge ten guidelines toward structure were set down, and various models are at present being constructed upon them; but the shape of union still seems to elude us. This suggests that nontheological questions may still be decisive for us.

Undoubtedly the path ahead will be accompanied by suspicions, fears, and hesitations, but we are moving forward. To be candid, there exists in Methodism something less than universal and uninterrupted enthusiasm for CO-

CU and for church union in general. Our very size makes us feel self-sufficient. Moreover, apathy is evident in all the constituencies; perhaps this is the worst problem. The information must get out; widespread involvement and debate must be encouraged; the most penetrating analysis and critical appraisal invited; the most earnest intercession sought. Because Methodists have insisted on this process they have been accused of "foot-dragging."

Hard questions, both theological and practical must be asked and painstakingly answered: Can freedom be balanced with unity? Is variety safeguarded? Is catholicity to be affirmed or is COCU contemplating a merely national church? Is provision made for preserving what is really valid within the various traditions? Can the integrity of each participating church be preserved? Does the proposed union look adequately beyond itself to other branches of the church? To the world? Is the plan sufficiently directed toward the *renewal* of the church as well as toward its unity? How, practically speaking, can it be made inclusive with regard to race and class? Have really adequate efforts been made to bring into the Consultation yet other traditions, particularly Lutherans and Baptists?

At the present moment the Consultation is seeking to perfect the Principles. In addition it is developing:

procedures to unite membership of the participating churches;

procedures to unite ministries of the participating churches;

structure and procedures for a Provisional Council.

These are all preludes to an early Plan of Union.

My own view is that we might best move forward in two stages with the intention of forming a more visible union: (1) Unite membership and ministries (Gal. 2:9). We should then have created a quite new ecumenical situation in the light of which we could take step (2), full organic union.

Now, given all I have said about Christian Unity, it does not necessarily argue for COCU. I am nevertheless hopeful and convinced that we shall not have completed this century without a drastic realignment of the churches in this country, and the COCU approach offers real promise. I am encouraged:

by what has happened in Rome.

by what has happened recently in the ancient Eastern Churches.

by what has happened in Orthodoxy.

by what has happened in Church of South India.

by what has happened in Geneva at the World Council of Churches.

73

by what has happened thus far in the Consultation.

I am encouraged by the conviction that an informed laity will be disposed to move more rapidly than the clergy. I am encouraged by the conviction that the prayer of our Lord that "they may all be one" will not forever go unanswered.

We have solid grounds for hope. Or shall the vision fade? Shall the tragedy of which W. H. Auden sings be ours too?

> Once again
> As in previous years we have seen the actual Vision and failed
> To do more than entertain it as an agreeable
> Possibility, once again we have sent Him away,
> Begging though to remain His disobedient servant,
> The promising child who cannot keep His word for long.[6]

There is a price to be paid, of course, but it is the price of the Cross. We will have to lose life to find it. There is a kind of eschatalogical dimension to our time, and some things cannot wait. This is one of them. Only one direction is open to us—forward. Therefore, let us in the words of Ephesians, "Spare no effort to make fast with bonds of peace the unity which the Spirit gives."

* *Collected Poetry.*

ministry
and mission

We have spoken much about ecumenism;
never just for the sake of ecumenism, but rather,
for the sake of the world—for the sake of mission. That mission and unity belong together is
the great ecumenical insight of the past twenty
years. At the 1952 meeting of the International
Missionary Council at Willingen, Germany, it
was stated:

The obligation to take the Gospel to the whole
world, and the obligation to draw all of God's people together, both rest upon Christ's whole work
and are indissolubly connected. Every attempt to
separate these tasks violates the wholeness of Christ's
ministry to the world.

We have so far spoken in lofty and laudable
terms about the church, its setting and its pros-

75

pects. As all of us know only too well there is another side of the story. The church in its ministry and its mission is faced with a major crisis as its critics both inside and outside its walls have been quick to point out. Much of this has been healthy. Often it has been overdone. I remain optimistic about the church, for my hope is in God.

One of the ablest and most articulate, and at the same time responsible critics was Samuel H. Miller, late dean of the Divinity School of Harvard University. He said:

We face three grave dangers. First, the major portion of the world in its interests, its motivations, its satisfactions, and its energies has pulled away from the Christian center. No amount of gallantry or amiable spoofing or Madison Avenue build-up can hide that fact from an honest man. The break has come; the great divorce is here. We have been disestablished from the governing nuclei whence men derive their motivation and their satisfaction.

Second, the vocabulary with which the Christian faith has spoken to the world from the beginning has lost its power. Symbols, rites, myths are as limp and strengthless as Dali's watches. They simply do not reverberate, resound, reach the quick of modern man. They are relics, emptied of their numinous charge. They change no one, provide no shock of reality, no access into living mystery. They are all explainable, historically conditioned, and have become furniture, not epiphany.

Finally, I see a "third force" of increasing power and magnitude, expressing itself in a variety of ways outside the church with little or no regard for organized religion. This is the renaissance of what might be called the religious question in the arts, in literature, and in some areas of science and industry.[1]

The crisis is particularly acute for many contemporary ministers, and has been for at least a decade. Too often the glory and the glow seem to have vanished from their ministry. For one thing, as we have seen, we dwell in an immensely changed world. It is, as has been emphasized, largely complex, technological, radically scientific, and secular in nature. The world is peopled by those who are often guilty, fearful, anxious, empty, despairing, and preoccupied. Some of them find their life's meaning in laboratories instead of temples. So great is man's admiration of his own achievements that he is reluctant to acknowledge God as the source of all good. What is the place of the parish ministry in such a setting? Yet the pastoral task has to be done precisely because of these factors. The aim of the ministry is clear: to make the Christian faith visible, intelligible, desirable. But the image of the ministry is blurred. Once the minister knew who he was. Now he is no longer sure.

[1] Excerpts from an address delivered in 1964 at the annual dinner of the Church Federation of Greater Chicago.

Ministers nowadays are caught in a web of tasks, some of them trivial in nature. "He may be asked," writes one, "in the course of a day to reweave a torn marriage, to give comfort to an aged man's fears, to laugh once again at a stale joke, to fix a roof, to operate a taxi service, to serve as baby sitter, to grind out endless material on a mimeograph machine, and then on a Sunday morning is expected to be a prophet of God!" No wonder the minister often feels torn, literally cut in small pieces. We can well appreciate the plaintive note of a village preacher in India, "I have discovered that I am a miscellaneous person."

Now this same sense of vocational uncertainty was experienced by the foreign missionary for at least ten years before it struck with any force in this country. It should not seem surprising that this should have been true. The pressure is always felt on what may be called the front line before it is felt along the supply routes and in the "zone of the interior." Now the front line is everywhere.

An interesting footnote to history is that it took eighteen hundred years for the Christian mission to reach around the world—the first movement of any kind to encircle the globe. In 1824 their farthest point of outreach was attained when the Franciscans established the last of their California missions at Sonora. That same year the Orthodox Russians, coming from the other direction, established a fur-trading post at nearby Fort Ross. They brought a missionary priest along. Eighteen centuries!

Yet that was near the beginning of the "great century" of missionary expansion, during the course of which and continuing through World War II missionaries—both Protestant and Roman Catholic—went wherever they could go, on all six continents and to the islands of the sea. The story is a well-nigh incredible one. One would not spontaneously think of Hegel as offering an accolade to missionaries, but when, near his death, he was told of their activities, he said: "This is the most significant event of our time." For thirty years I have followed this movement and its history closely, have been deeply involved in it. I know its accomplishments and I know its weaknesses, shortcomings, and problems very well. Yet I must conclude that the Christian missionary undertaking, for sheer boldness of spirit, heroism, selfless dedication, and high achievement against overwhelming odds, for wholehearted obedience to the gospel, for the building up of people, is without parallel in history. We can only marvel and thank God for it. Its critics are many, and large numbers of persons even in the countries that have most benefitted by the efforts have not hesitated to disparage their work. Yet the most sensitive spirits—Christian and non-Christian—have acknowledged their positive contributions. One such person is the poet, Leopold Senghor, president of Senegal, who wrote of the missionary:

Bless this people who have brought me your good news
Lord, and opened my heavy lids to the light of faith.
They have opened my heart to knowledge of the world,
  showing me the rainbow of my brothers' faces.

Yet when all this has been said, the fact remains that at the very time of the greatest geographical extension, the missionary enterprise has been called most sorely into question and has been overtaken by great uncertainty. It is a little reminiscent of Reinhold Niebuhr's theme in *The Irony of American History:* at the precise time the United States becomes a world power, the world has become a peculiarly inhospitable place for a world power. This does not mean that either a great nation or the missionary movement can renounce its responsibility.

Even the old missionary symbols have lost their power. Livingstone's appealing image of "the smoke of 10,000 villages in which the name of Christ was not known" no longer grasps hold of us who live under the threat of mushroom-shaped clouds! In a word, for a score of years there has been a serious problem of morale for missionaries, and missions have been in doubt; there is hesitation and loss of momentum. Roman Catholic and Protestant analyses of the situation are similar.

James Stewart attributes the decline in missionary zeal to four factors: "the chilly shadow of intellectual doubt," "self-distrust," "the break-up of the once familiar patterns of the missionary enterprise," and finally, "assimilation to the world." [2]

Decline in missionary morale is undoubtedly a complex matter. Some factors are simply a part of being a missionary in any age. It is never an easy task. I am reminded that a man once observed to the editor of *Punch* that the magazine was not as funny as it used to be. The editor replied that it never was! So with the missionary task: it is not easy today and never was. So also with the pastoral ministry. I mean, the fact that the missionary is a marked person, a representative person, often seen as playing an absurd role. I mean the problems of loneliness, isolation, climate, language, the necessity of identification with an alien people, and so on. *All these one can endure.*

A second factor is worldwide disturbance—China, Cuba, Algeria, Congo; the list is long.

[2] Cf. Stewart, *Thine Is the Kingdom* (New York: Scribner's, 1957), pp. 18-19.

The "closed doors," the difficulty to get visas, the insecurity at times. *These also one can endure.* Indeed, all these and more are *given,* for as Jesus said, "In the world you will have tribulation."

Another factor is the prevailing attitude toward the West. Americans, especially, like to be liked, but this pleasant experience is not always available to the missionary. He may be the butt of jokes—not just because he is a missionary but because he is, say, an American. But extreme nationalism can be difficult. Likewise, Western ways can also be exasperating to the Asian or African. Hear this poem by an African:

Hurray for those who never invented anything;
Hurray for those who never explored anything;
Hurray for those who never conquered anything;
Hurray for Joy!
Hurray for Love!
Hurray for Incarnate Tears!

All this the missionary can endure. The day-to-day tensions, the pressures, and the frustrations, often accentuated by the very factors I have mentioned, *these too the missionary can endure.*

Perhaps the clearest and most penetrating analysis of the morale factor of missionaries was made by the late Professor Walter Freytag. When once he spoke of changes experienced by the modern missionary, the first, he said, was *limitation*. "The sphere of work of Western missionaries is becoming limited." The second change he characterized as *"lost directness."* In other words, the missionary is in so many cases removed farther and farther from the scene of action. The third change he called the *"endangered image,"* the "blurred image," "the loss of that conception of ourselves which guides us consciously or, even more, unconsciously." [3] In such situations the whole existence and integrity of the missionary may be called into question. *This one cannot long endure* without renewal of spiritual resources and renewed understanding of one's role. Deep, long-continued anxiety and loss of clear role robs one of his sense of humor, his sense of proportion, his sense of vocation, thus destroying his very weapons of combat.

This analysis of missionary morale may be of some help in understanding the vocational crisis experienced by many ministers and priests in this country today. With the pastor too, in the final analysis, the root problem is loss of clarity of role and image of the ministry and mission of which he is a part. There exists as a part of the picture problems in recruitment both for the

[3] In speech given in Accra, Ghana, at Ghana Assembly of International Missionary Council, January, 1958, "Changes in the Patterns of Western Missions," *The Ghana Assembly of the International Missionary Council*, ed. Ronald K. Orchard (London: Edinburgh House Press, 1958), pp. 138 ff.

pastoral ministry as well as for missionary service. It is often pointed out that just at the time of this crisis, present-day youth are committing themselves to the Peace Corps and other types of missions that are secularly oriented. It may well be that this fact will afford the church occasion to rediscover what its own distinctive role is. The road to recovery would appear to be precisely to attempt to regain clarity regarding ministry and mission. This process, I believe, is already well under way.

The first observation that must be made concerning Christian ministry is that the church in our day is recovering the glory of servanthood— a servanthood that is freighted with the meaning given it by the One whom the church acknowledges as Lord. As Bonhoeffer once wrote: "The Church is her true self only when she exists for humanity." Our perspective is that the church's ministry is Christ's ministry and that the whole ministry is given to the whole church. It follows that each member has a part in this ministry. All Christians are missional people; that is, they are sent to witness and serve.

Søren Kirkegaard said that the best way to keep church people from becoming Christians is to have them assume the *name* of Christian and stop there. But the Christian may *not* stop there. He is called to faith and commitment. He must assume a share in the responsibility for the whole world that has been given to the whole church. Such a total view is seen clearly in the New Testament. The one ministry has a variety of forms that unitedly make up the service of the church. As Israel was a nation of priests, so the early church, seeing itself as the New Israel, was "a royal priesthood."

Israel, too, had variations in its one ministry. The whole people were chosen of God, not just as favored ones but as those called to special responsibility. From among the whole populace, an elite was selected to represent in a special manner the presence and activity of God in the nation and the world. The king represented God's rule. The prophet was the discerner and interpreter of God's action in history, a foreseer who was constantly calling the people to attention in the light of God's judgment and mercy: he called them back that he might direct them forward. Israel always had remembrance of the story of Exodus, the Word-Event of their history, which was a reminder that the One they met in their extremity was one who cared for and delivered his people. That is the way God is; that is the way he acts. The prophets interpreted history Exodus-wise. The priests administered in sacred things; by rite and ceremony they celebrated what it meant to be God's humble, thankful, and dedicated people, so that life might never be robbed of its transcendent dimension and mystery. The priesthood was extended so that the father of a family exercised the priestly function in that circle.

The church learned much from Israel's model of the ministry. It continued in its life the one ministry—kingly, priestly, and prophetic. Moreover, it saw this threefold unitary ministry fulfilled and exemplified in the work of the Lord. He is commonly thought of as prophet, priest, and king. His words, deeds, and being remarkably confirm one another. All three sustain and proclaim his Lordship.

Though we have affirmed that the whole ministry belongs to the whole church, in all reality it must be confessed that the whole church does not accept this responsibility. Therefore, individuals and groups have repeatedly arisen who have understood this and have called the church once again to assume its responsibility before God and for mankind. Their ministry is based on the expenditure of themselves, or, better, on the "cruciform principle." In what superficially may seem a waste of life, they find the very meaning of human existence. This should not be surprising in view of the fact that the central symbol of the Christian faith is the Cross: what seems manifestly meaningless is in reality the intensification of meaning. As Israel recalls the Exodus-event, so Christians recall the Christ-Event. This is the way God is; this is the way he acts. As Bernard of Clairvaux stated it: "The cross remains, while the world turns." As the Jew thinks Exodus-wise, the Christian both thinks and acts "Cross-wise."

The pages of history are crowded with such figures. They are the ones who forsake brilliant careers for obscure service, who literally waste their lives for others, who risk everything with hardly a hint that they are risking anything. These are the ones who go to the far places and the deep places and the out-of-the-way places. These are the ones we forget, or if we remember them at all, it is only to wonder why they do what they do. The writer of Hebrews describes them as those of whom "the world is not worthy." Or they are called "fools for Christ's sake," the "weak," "Christ's underlings," "like men condemned to death in the arena," "hungry, thirsty and in rags," "a spectacle to the whole universe," "sharers in the sufferings of Christ." They are the ones who give reality to the fact that the whole ministry is exacted of the whole church, and in proof of this they reproduce the ministry of Christ before the eyes of both the church and the world. They "act out" the gospel and make it believable. In Robert Frost's rendering of Job in *A Masque of Reason*

87

he has God say in response to Job's complaint at his having to be a "spectacle" before men:

> It had to be at somebody's expense.
> Society can never think things out:
> It has to see them acted out by actors,
> Devoted actors at a sacrifice—
> The ablest actors I can lay my hands on.

The ministry of the whole church for the whole world is understood and executed in a twofold manner. The first task is that of "justing love"; the other is "witnessing love."

By "justing love" I mean insistence on justice in the social order and working toward it wherever we are by means open to us. This does not have to do in the main with face-to-face relations and direct alleviation of human need. It is the way of loving one's brother whom he has *not* seen, the creation of an atmosphere in which immediate needs may be relieved. It presses beyond kindness to justice.

"Witnessing love" is of a different kind. It is face-to-face love—*agape*. While one is busily engaged in giving himself for mankind, either in the earning of his livelihood or pursuing efforts which express "just love," there are interruptions. One is confronted with human need in one of its numberless guises. Here is an occasion for directly relieving distress and for declaring the Word, or for making it believable by the deed of kindness. While the awakened man digs ditches, works on a legal brief, attends to a suffering patient, he may at the same time be busy at being a priest—declaring forgiveness, announcing that men are free to live, calling them out of their "tombs" into life. In other words, while engaged in doing the *deed* of the gospel, the deed that confronts him to be done, he declares the Word of the gospel.

Let us put the whole matter in a slightly different setting. The church, as it comes into being wherever two or three are gathered together in the name of Jesus, is the new community or new fellowship (*koinonia*) of those who have found new being in experiencing Jesus Christ as Lord. That very fellowship, insofar as it demonstrates oneness and the evident reconciling power of God in Jesus Christ, is itself a witness. It addresses itself to the world in two ways: by preaching of the gospel (*kerygma*), and by acts of humble, loving service (*diakonia*).

Such a twofold ministry involves every Christian. This should be evident for those of us who are of Protestant rootage, for we are in the heritage of the "priesthood of all believers." Every Christian has a *priestly* ministry. We should note that this fact has never been entirely lost in Roman Catholicism. It is now being recovered by the whole church.

Traditionally we have thought spontaneously

of the clergy when we have heard reference to the ministry. Naturally clergy has its important share in the ministry, but it is by no means the whole of it. The clergy no longer may occupy the center of the stage. For a long period this was possible. The very term "clergy" comes from *cleros*, which means "magistrate." Once the parson—literally, the *person*—was the best educated and very often the most important individual in the community. This is no longer necessarily true—as any preacher can testify from looking out over his congregation on a Sunday morning.

The stage was reached when in both Protestantism and Roman Catholocism the clergy *were* the church. Protestants have more readily seen this in Rome than in their own case, but it has been true among us as well. Somehow the clergy came to the place of doing the theologizing for the laity; they did the "faithing" for them. The clergy were seen as doing their best to "protect" the laity from the world.

We are now offered an exact reversal of the former conception. We now see the clergy enabling the laity to be the church. Rather than protecting the laity from the world, the role of the clergy is to equip the layman *for* the world. We could say that the clergyman's primary ministry is in the church and the layman's in the world.

90

This is not just good theory, which it is; or good New Testament teaching, which it is; this is the way things are structured. The clergy are not scattered in the world, nor indeed can they be. In fact, they are the least prepared for this, as laymen themselves constantly affirm. The laymen are now seen not only as the front-line troops; they are a body assigned to *be* the church in mission in the world. This mission they can fulfill not as isolated units, but corporately. Each member has his part to be a delegate of the whole church where he is; the whole church brought to focus at a particular point. All members are, as Luther put it, "little Christs" to their neighbors.

The ways of providence are indeed fearful and wonderful. The traditional role of the clergy bearing the *whole* ministry of the church is largely outlived. This role no longer fits, but the continued effort to make it fit accounts in large part for the malaise of many preachers—especially the younger ones. But once the ministry of Christ is seen as belonging to the whole church and the role of the ministry of the laity is clarified, the role of the clergy may also be clarified and rectified. Obviously this may be a painful process; but until it is accomplished the crisis in vocation and recruitment will not be relieved. It is a problem and responsibility of the whole church—Protestant and Roman

Catholic. Bishop Otto Dibelius used to say that the shortage of clergy is a judgment upon the church.

The new cleric will, first of all, be teacher to a far larger degree than has been the case in the past. He will use every occasion and every means open to him for this purpose. For example, his preaching will give more emphasis to instruction. Repeated studies show that the average layman is neither informed about the Christian faith, nor, according to his own admission, is he guided by it to any great extent in his daily decisions. This situation must be corrected, and soon. This implies new responsibilities for our seminaries. Increasingly the pastor will engage in an "equipping ministry." As it were, he will meet the "troops"—the laymen—at the door of the church (for the weight of being free men in the world drives them back), "wash their feet," instruct them, lead them in meaningful worship that renews them for further encounter, and send them back into the world of everydayness to continue their ministry. His role is to help them "live their baptism."

Second, the pastor-teacher must be pastor-priest. All Christians have this role, but the cleric has it in a representative sense. As Jesus was among us as servant, so must his followers be.

Third, the pastor-teacher and pastor-priest must be pastor-leader. It is as if he were a leader of the troops. He is called upon to be an example of what a man *is* in the twentieth century. He is shepherd of a kind of revolutionary cadre which takes seriously its task of changing the world. He spends himself on behalf of his people. The blurred image of minister and missionary is becoming clearer again. It bears the shape of a cross. If this is the shape of the ministry, then by definition, pastors and missionaries of every age are robbed of the right to be frustrated!

Jesus Christ was the model of ministry for both laity and clergy. He is Teacher, Servant, Sacrifice. So in our own way must we, his followers, be. Together, clergy and laity form a corporate ministry that plans strategy, finds resources, and carries out the ministry of Christ among men.

Already in discussing ministry we have anticipated the new meaning of mission. The New Testament abounds in images of the church—nearly a hundred different ones: the people of God, the body of Christ, the fellowship of the Holy Spirit, the household of faith. Speaking in the very broadest terms, during the early centuries the church's image was that of eschatalogical congregation. It was a "colony of heaven," a kind of beachhead in this world and also in the world to come. The medieval church saw itself as universal hierarchical order. A third compre-

hensive image of the church came with the Reformers—prophetic community of the Word.
In each case the church has tended to turn in on
itself in self-satisfaction or self-preservation. Its
salt is not for self-preservation; it is the salt of
the earth. It is not a cult of self-enlightenment;
it is the light of the world. It is not a loaf; it is
leaven.

The church exists for the world. So it is that
today we see more clearly than ever before that
the church *is* mission; it is sent of God for the
sake of the world. The mission of the church is
seen as the mission of the Triune God. It is
working with him. Out of the depths of his love
for all men, the Father has sent forth his Son to
reconcile all things to himself, that we and all
men might, through the Spirit, be made one in
him with the Father in that perfect love which
is the very nature of God.

A speaker at the great meeting of the International Missionary Council gathered at Willingen, Germany in 1952, said that theologically
the mission of the church is like a "divine relay
race"—the Father sends the Son, the Father and
Son send the Holy Spirit, the Triune God sends
the church, and the church sends the people to
witness and serve. The mission of the church is
seen as the work of God in Christ, through the
whole church, by the power of the Holy Spirit,
for all men throughout the whole world. A sec-

ular definition of mission might be: the true humanization of all mankind. Or from the Nicene Creed: one holy catholic and *apostolic* Church.

In the light of this understanding of mission, certain derivative insights are available to us:

1. There is only one basis for mission that will stand the test of the devastating developments that are so evident in many parts of the world today. It is an overwhelming sense of gratitude to God for his goodness and mercy shown to us by his grace in Jesus Christ our Lord. Therefore it must be shared.

2. We have come to a period of emphasis on depth of mission. Teilhard de Chardin uses an exciting metaphor as he contrasts the geometric figures of plane and sphere. A plane is limitless and therefore cannot ever be covered. The surface of a sphere, however, is by definition limited. It can be covered, like the paint advertised as covering the earth. Once covered it cannot be any more covered except in depth. So it is with the Christian mission. Geographically the gospel has been carried wherever it could be throughout the earth. We must turn now to the more significant dimension of depth.

3. Emphasis, too, must be made on the "mission of the presence," as the Brothers of the Taizé Community would call it. This takes seriously the promise of our Lord to be where two

or three of his followers are gathered in his name. Where he is served, there he is Lord, and a non-Christian atmosphere is transformed into a Christian one.

4. "Missions" have been replaced by *mission*. Involvement in it is no longer an option, but is an obligation for the Christian. It is not what someone else does *there*; but what *we* do here, there, and everywhere. It is a concern not of the few but of the many, of all. To be Christian is a matter not merely of privilege but of responsibility.

Since the church *is* mission, we should expect this fact to be evident in each congregation. This is the emphasis of the World Council of Churches study of the recent past concerning "The Missionary Structure of the Congregation." It comes to focus on "the congregation *for others*." It raises direct and hard questions on how the congregation can restructure itself in worship, study, and training for the task of mission that lies at its own doors and beyond. To guide the congregation in its task, the study asks, "How can we recognize—in the flower shop, at the street-car stop, in the slums of big cities, in the cinema, in the picket line—that same Christ, whose body we have shared at the Lord's table?"

One is impressed at the number of experimental ministries across our country where these perspectives are being taken seriously; where once again congregations are finding themselves in mission, learning to celebrate the gospel and to interpret the mighty acts of God in the past and present within its own life and to reach out in service and witness to the community in which it finds itself. Years ago Reinhold Niebuhr observed that "The renewal of the Church demanded of us now must . . . include encounter with the sins of the community." And Albert Camus joins him with this word:

The world of today needs Christians who remain Christians. What the world expects of Christians is that they should speak out, loud and clear, and that they should voice their condemnation in such a way that never a doubt, never the slightest doubt, could arise in the heart of the simplest man. That they should get away from abstractions and confront the bloodstained face history has taken on today.[4]

So the congregation for others gathers with the service of worship of God and scatters in service of men. Such was the early church at its best.

We have tried to stress that when we become clear about *the* ministry of the church, we can once again speak more clearly about the ordained or representative ministry. In the same

[4] In an address entitled "The Unbeliever and Christians" delivered to a group of French Christians.

way, when we become clearer about *the* mission of the church, we can address ourselves to missions and the role of missionary. We can use the term "missions" as referring primarily to that part of the mission of the church which reaches beyond the immediate scope of service of a local congregation and which the local congregation will fulfill in concert with others. The missionary crosses the boundaries of his home parish to engage in the work of mission in another parish across the city or across the world.

We may speak meaningfully of *the* mission of the church *urbi et orbi*—to the city and to the world. If we had had any doubts about the need of focus upon the city, we have had many vivid reminders of this need in the scores of urban centers across our country that have erupted during recent summers.

Soon after the tragic riot there I had occasion to be in Detroit and was shown through that startled city. It was deeply scarred by civil disorder; one almost says civil strife! What surprised me most was the extent, for the marks of violence were scattered over an area measuring some twelve miles by eighteen miles. Within this territory there were literally thousands of fires and thousands more of fire alarms. Though destruction appeared at times to have been wanton, visited on white and black alike, it seemed to be not entirely indiscriminate but strangely selective. Apparently memory is long when it comes to long-endured exploitation or supposed exploitation by price gouging and overcharging. Violence seemed to be visited especially where these practices were alleged. Naturally, the baser elements and habitual criminals took advantage of the situation. Naturally, also, multitudes of the innocent suffered. Yet hundreds of people who were not by habit criminal were swept along by mob spirit.

Nor were all the participants of one race only. White and Negro alike were involved, and people from both communities indulged in looting, violence, and destruction.

Those who are competent to judge call it not merely a race riot but a racial upheaval with strong economic overtones. Once such venom is released, it seems to know neither bonds nor restraint. All I can say is that block after gruesome block of Detroit resembled nothing so much as the pictures one has often seen of the ruins of French and Belgian villages after the devastation of World War I. Even so, there is an irony in the fact that this catastrophe should have overtaken Detroit, whose slums are far from the worst our country offers and whose record in race relations had been among the best.

The question obviously comes to us: Why? It is all too easy to say that we do not know why. Would not it be far more truthful to confess

that we do know? A half dozen years ago Dr. James B. Conant, former president of Harvard University, warned us that we were allowing "social dynamite" to accumulate in our cities. Its ingredients were overcrowded ghettos, educational dropouts, unemployment of Negro youths far out of proportion to that prevailing among their white counterparts, careful containment of socially unacceptable people, filthy streets, miserable housing infested with rats, abysmally low self-esteem on the part of those who live there. What a fertile soil for the demogogue to grow in! To tolerate these conditions, while at the same time despising constructive Negro leaders, is to become responsible for creating the extremists.

Then there was the breakdown of communication. So it is that a recent article in the *New York Times* magazine bore the title: "Whitey Hasn't Got the Message." Selma, Alabama, did not get it over to us. The meaning of Watts did not really get through to us. Did we suppose that James Baldwin's book *The Fire Next Time* was merely an exercise in poetic license and literary exaggeration? If we got around to reading *The Autobiography of Malcolm X*, did we merely conclude that he was an unpleasant person, or did it teach us that so far we have only been playing with the race issue in this country? The fact is that "Whitey" has not yet got the message. And if we do not get it, let's face it: there's more of the same and worse than Detroit ahead for us!

What then must we do? If healing is to be found, the Christian, white or black, will assume a full measure of responsibility for what has happened across our land. This is the pathway toward redemption. Did not Jesus redeem mankind precisely by identifying himself fully with sinful men? He did not love only those who loved him; he loved and forgave even those who crucified him. In identifying himself with every man he identified himself with the very love of God. At one and the same time he showed us what God is like and what we must be like. He died not for righteous men but for sinners. As all men, without any exception, are equal in God's sight, so they must all be seen as acceptable in God's sight. Thus Jesus showed forth true love in sharing the purpose of God in loving all men and hating none. He bids us also to love our enemies—without exception—to bless, to pray for them.

Our summons, then, is to assume responsibility for what has happened in Detroit and clear across our nation. We are to assume responsibility for evil in the world. In doing so we identify ourselves with the least person for whom Christ died. This is the road that transforms hurt to healing. Here is the sure way of

101

salvation. Here also is our mission to the city, calling for an all-out commitment as citizens and as Christians to transform our cities in the name of Christ.

Our mission must also be to the world. It is thus a sign that God has acted for the whole world, and so must we. But our approach nowadays must be different. Just as Christian missions to the city must be comprehensive, the same is true in any other part of the world. Let me try to illustrate this by Africa for a moment. It is, of course, a vast area, full of variety, full of vitality. I recall some words cited by D. T. Niles about a Christian hospital in Africa. "A Christian hospital is not Christian simply by being a hospital; it is only Christian when it is part of a total approach to the problems of African life." This is true, to some degree, everywhere, but more so in Africa, where there is so much wholeness to the social fabric.

What might be an approach that would take this into consideration? During a visit to Africa three years ago I endeavored to formulate the questions that might well guide the missionary task. They might well be adopted to any situation:

1. What is the historical memory? What event stands out? When this is discovered, if it can be, then the action of God is shown through that event. The gospel is retold in terms of it.

102

This is not new. For example, Paul in Romans interpreted the meaning of Abraham in terms of faith and as the father of all men of faith. The Gospel of Mark interprets Moses in terms of a New Exodus. The Gospel of Luke reinterprets the creation in terms of the New Creation. How can African culture or any culture be reinterpreted in terms of its great historical memory?

2. What is the basic understanding of life? What do men take for granted? What, for instance, are their ethical norms? One African suggested these five: loyalty, cooperation, endurance, self-control, sacrifice. He rejected many other norms as less applicable in African society. The evangelistic task would then be to deny these, insofar as they are idolatrous, and then affirm them. For all the promises of God have their "Yes" in Jesus Christ. God plants the seed and brings forth the fruit.

3. What is their basic search? Their ultimate question? This then is their salvation-question. For example, ask an African what he really wants, and he is likely to say: "Land, health, education, economic welfare, freedom." But these are not his real wants, for one can probe behind these and ask, "Why?" As one pushes further and further back he comes to something very like this: He wants *dignity*. If this is the salvation-question, the gospel is always addressed to it—deep unto deep.

103

These searching questions suggest in at least a fragmentary way an approach in depth to the task of mission in our day. In the past none of us were so conscious of these things. God seems to have blessed our efforts anyway. Now, however, we are in a deeply self-conscious era. Our mission must be in deeper terms and more comprehensive terms if we are to address the whole world in the name of Jesus Christ.

The task is difficult and the future uncertain. This very uncertainty, though, is the exciting part about the mission of the church. It invites the continuing journey of faith upon which our Father Abraham embarked. We, too, may with prayerful confidence venture forward in mission.

worship and the church's mission

Worship is a problem for modern man—even for the practicing Christian. It is no news to any of us that the prayer closet is not as much used nowadays as once it was. This is not solely because of the rapid pace of life or the many demands made upon us or our distractions. Chiefly it is because of the fact that for multitudes of people, worship, whether private or public, has lost much of its meaning. We may as well acknowledge this from the outset. Paul Tillich said not long before his death that the revelatory experience is very thin at present—that we are a "waiting people" before God.

At the same time, the man of faith is aware that God is showing himself mightily at work both in the contemporary world and in the church. He is giving us a new world and a new church for a new world—before our very eyes he seems to be renewing his church with regard to its unity, its theology, the ministry of its laity, and finally, with regard to its liturgy. This is occurring right across denominational boundaries and with such a universality and such a simultaneity that the man of faith, I say, can only conclude that this is none other than the work of the Spirit of God in our midst. This renewal of the church, it cannot too often be emphasized, must not be understood as being for the sake of the church; rather, it is for the sake of the world, for mission in the world.

But what is the mission of the church? It is the mission of God; it is that all men may believe and know that they are accepted entirely by the One who placed them here, and who has sent his Son to save them. It was for this that Jesus prayed (John 17). This the Christian learns in childhood when he memorizes John 3:16. The mission of the church is directed toward the true humanization of all mankind, so fulfilling God's purpose in his creation of man. This is what God both permits and empowers in Jesus Christ. This is but one way of expressing the meaning of mission, but I believe it to be consistent with the whole tenor of New Testament religion. Another way of putting it, though we seldom express it this way nowadays, is that the

106

gospel affirms that man is of supreme worth before God. Jesus Christ, and all that attaches to him, and all that he has done for men, is a guarantee of this worth.

Just here, then, let me say a preliminary word about worship. One of the root meanings of the word, as we have all been told, is literally, *worth-ship*. When he is confronted by the mighty acts of the One who is himself all-worthy, man's own worth is finally seen. The root meaning of worship, however, is better understood from the Old English word *weorthan*, to become, to come to be. In worship man enters into his real being, his true humanity before the One who both gives him life and limits his life. Perhaps Jonathan Edwards had something like this in view when he defined worship as "consent to Being."

We have now said two apparently contradictory things: that worship is a problem to the present-day Christian, and that the church is being renewed in worship *for mission*. The qualifying phrase "for mission" is decisive. For worship and mission belong together. That is the thesis of this chapter. If they can be seen as belonging together, and kept together, then we can look for fuller recovery of both worship and mission in a meaningful way, and worship will cease to be a problem of the magnitude it has now become. On the other hand, when "discontinuity" occurs between them there is in some sense a denial of both worship and mission. This is always detrimental to the total life of the church.

Worship and mission belong together, first of all, because of the very nature of worship. Basically it means to bow down in submission and homage to the one to whom supreme honor is due. It is, as Evelyn Underhill has expressed it, "the response of the creature to the Eternal." For God has the initiative; it is for man to respond to him. The first commandment is: "You shall have no other gods before me." But the Ten Commandments are prefaced by the words: "I am the Lord your God, who brought you out of the land of Egypt, out of the house of bondage." It is the God who has delivered whom we are to obey. John Calvin once said that "true worship consists in obedience alone."

Worship, then, is not in isolation, a passing attitude to be experienced at particular times and places. Rather, for Christians worship is seen in the context of total response to the action of God in Christ in the totality of their existence. So it is that worship and mission are not to be compartmentalized. They are different aspects of one relationship—acknowledgment of God and obedience to him on the part of the whole church. It is a participation in the work of God. William Temple once declared that worship is "to quicken the conscience by the holiness of

God, to feed the mind by the truth of God, to purge the imagination by the beauty of God, to open up the heart to the love of God, *to devote the will to the purpose of God.*"

God has the initiative in seeking men to worship him in spirit and in truth, just as Christ came to seek and to save the lost. What is it to "worship in spirit," if it is not to gather up all there is of us and to appear before him as we are? For the spirit is that point at which our whole being comes together. In the final analysis men can appear as they really are only before God and before no other. In a real sense we have nothing to offer him that is entirely our own except our sins. One of the characters in Kazantzakis' *The Greek Passion* says: "I've nothing to sacrifice to God, and yet it still torments me to sacrifice that nothing."

And what is it to "worship in truth" but to do so in accordance with the truth about God and the truth about ourselves, both of which have been made manifest in Jesus Christ the Truth? It is to respond with sincerity and to pray according to the real nature of God, whose nature is to have concern for all his creatures. To worship in spirit and in truth is not to change God but for men to be changed—it is for them "to come to be" men. Thus our call is not just a call to a life of *prayer*, but a call to *life* which participates in the work of God.

109

Now, all this is set within the context of community—the church that has itself occurred in response to what has occurred in Jesus Christ. Indeed, very early the church understood itself to be the body of Christ, and this experience taught it, as H. Richard Niebuhr has said, that "to believe is to be united with both the one in whom one believes and with all those who believe in him." Christian worship, whether private or public, is always corporate, and liturgy is quite literally the work of God's people. It is always in behalf of the world. All this is seen, for example, in the Lord's Prayer, which is surely communal and corporate and full of concern for the real world. Edmund Schlink has observed that worship is "the life-giving center of the Church's activity in the world." When it is genuine it "breaks out into the world, and the whole life of the members becomes that sacrifice of praise that is extolled by Christ." Moreover, worship and mission were brought together as they were embodied in Jesus Christ, and this unity was continued when two or three gathered together in his name experienced his presence.

The Witness of the Scriptures

The view that worship and mission belong together is abundantly supported by the Scriptures. The people of God are a holy people whose mission is found in their very meaning which is celebrated when they gather together for worship. That Israel was a covenant community whose history places the people under obligation is seen repeatedly in the Old Testament, but nowhere any more movingly than in Deuteronomy 6:

"When your son asks you in time to come, 'What is the meaning of the testimonies and the statutes and the ordinances which the Lord our God has commanded you?' then you shall say to your son, 'We were Pharaoh's slaves in Egypt; and the Lord brought us out of Egypt with a mighty hand . . . that he might bring us in and give us the land which he swore to give to our fathers. And the Lord commanded us to do all these statutes . . . for our good always. (Deut. 6:20 24 RSV.)

The early Christians likewise understood themselves to be "a chosen race, a royal priesthood, a dedicated nation . . . the people of God."

Or again, the classic experience of the prophet Isaiah in the Temple did not end there. Rather its culmination was in his being sent forth into a real and harsh world, there to speak for the One whom he had met in the sanctuary. Or consider how the psalms never cease to call to worship but always within view of the real world.

In the New Testament it is notable that all four of the Gospels end on notes that combine

111

worship and mission. Luke is particularly notable in this respect. His first volume, the Gospel,
is thoroughly liturgical in its mood and content;
one might almost say that it is also liturgical in
its structure. It both begins and ends in the
Temple. His second volume, the Acts of the
Apostles, also begins in the Temple but pro-
ceeds as an account of magnificent missionary
obedience. In all four of the great hymns of the
church that the Third Evangelist records at the
beginning of his narrative, the dual notes of
response to God and of responsibility for men
are sounded. For example, the *Benedictus* begins with praise of God but closes with phrases
that refer to the needs of men: the forgiveness of
sins, the compassion of God, light for darkness,
guidance toward peace.

The Fourth Gospel is likewise thoroughly liturgical in nature, as Oscar Cullmann has made
so abundantly clear.[1] Constantly sacramental, it
is at the same time, and for this very reason,
constantly thrusting toward real life. Indeed, it
is both implicitly and explicitly the offer of life
—of true humanity—and therefore speaks directly to life; and, incidentally, to no age does
it speak more directly than to our own. Someone
recently observed that Matthew may be best expressed by medieval art but John by modern art.

[1] *Early Christian Worship* (London: SCM Press, 1953).

Turning again to Acts we see how it literally breathes liturgy and life. At the very beginning Luke tells us, "They met constantly to hear the apostles teach, and to share the common life, to break bread, and to pray" (Acts 2:42 NEB). Or again we read: "With one mind they kept up their daily attendance at the temple, and, breaking bread in private houses, shared their meals with unaffected joy, as they praised God and enjoyed the favour of the whole people. And day by day the Lord added to their number those whom he was saving" (Acts 2:46-47 NEB). Or again: "And every day they went steadily on with their teaching in the temple and in private houses, telling the good news of Jesus the Messiah" (Acts 5:42 NEB). In Acts 13 is an account of the wonderful little church at Antioch that was later to contribute so much to liturgical history. The record of the genesis at Antioch of the mission to the Gentiles is significant: "While they were worshiping the Lord and fasting, the Holy Spirit said, 'Set apart for me Barnabas and Saul for the work to which I have called them.' Then after fasting and praying they laid their hands on them and sent them off. So, being sent out by the Holy Spirit, they went down to Seleucia; and from there they sailed to Cyprus." (Acts 13:2-4 RSV.)

One might also refer to the Epistles, which not only arose out of the mission but are them-

113

selves liturgical and as such supportive of the mission. Moreover, from earliest times they were used liturgically by the churches.

The Witness of Church History

So the early church went on its way rejoicing as it followed the road of missionary obedience. We, in our day, have forgotten how to celebrate. Someone has observed that "our worship services are a mixture of sermon, seminar in sacred music and excerpts from liturgical history." Not so the first Christians. They celebrated the meaning of their faith, new life in Christ, and the joy of the resurrection, so much so that, as Tertullian reminds us, the Christians never fasted or knelt in prayer on the Lord's Day. Then they could stand upright like men and rejoice! Very early the modes of worship assumed forms recognizable by us. Ignatius of Antioch, who as bishop was "master of liturgy," writes during the first half of the second century of services in which there were readings from the prophets, from Matthew and the Epistles, a homily, hymns, and prayers. Frequently he also refers to the Eucharist. Sometimes there was an offering for the needy. During the same century the writings of Justin Martyr and the *Didache* confirm the same patterns. The *Didache* speaks also of catechetical instruction, though the catechumens were excluded from Holy Communion itself. Justin Martyr says that "after our baptism and first communion, we continued to remind each other of them," a foretaste of one of our contemporaries who speaks of communion helping us to "live our baptism."

The Lord's Supper or the Eucharist therefore very early became central to the church's life. How central it was is suggested by the many "dining room scenes" recorded in the Gospels, which are surely sacramental touches. The local churches clearly received this rite as a part of their evangelization, as Paul indicates in writing to the Christians at Corinth: "For the tradition which I handed on to you came to me from the Lord himself: that the Lord Jesus, on the night of his arrest, took bread and, after giving thanks to God, broke it and said: 'This is my body, which is for you; do this as a memorial for me'" (I Cor. 11:23-24 NEB). The service at one and the same time points backward in recollection to the crucified and risen historical Jesus; it points forward in anticipation to the summing up of all things in Christ; it points to the real presence of the Lord of the church, who stands in the midst of the community of the faithful. This liturgy of the Lord's Supper is something to be *done*, not just to be heard and seen. It is the real work of the people of God. Moreover, there is an intimate relationship between the

115

"Do this" of the Eucharist and the "Go ye" to the Dominical command to mission.

Has ever a command been so thoroughly obeyed as the "Do this"? There has never been a day since Pentecost in which Christians have not met together to celebrate and commemorate the death and resurrection of Jesus Christ. And when they have done so, they have experienced once again precisely what no one can do for himself—that is, forgive his own sins. They know that this God has graciously done for them through our Lord Jesus Christ.

One cannot consider Eucharist in our day without expressing a debt of gratitude to Dom Gregory Dix and particularly for his great book *The Shape of the Liturgy*. He emphasizes the fourfold shape of the service of Holy Communion: (1) the "taking" of the offering of bread and wine; (2) the prayer of thanksgiving; (3) the breaking of the loaf; and (4) the giving of the elements to the communicants. Whatever the variations expressed in the different traditions, these four are invariable.

Our emphasis, however, is that these stages not only constitute the form of the liturgy but also outline the basic style of the Christian life. For is not the Lord's Supper a kind of "acted parable" of Christian living? Is not our understanding of life a receiving, an attitude of thanksgiving, a breaking or offering of ourselves

116

for mankind, thereby sharing of our very lives with our fellowmen? No wonder Dix called the Eucharist "an entire epitome of the Gospel." The Archbishop of Canterbury, Michael Ramsey, says that "the Liturgy declares the Gospel of God." In so saying he has Paul on his side, for the apostle wrote to the Corinthians, "For every time you eat this bread and drink the cup, you *proclaim* the death of the Lord, until he comes." The sacrament is a preaching! Furthermore, Bishop John A. T. Robinson observes that following communion "the sharing of bread, concluded now sacramentally, must be continued socially—and thence economically and politically." Worship and mission belong together!

The Eastern tradition has been more faithful to this insight than the Western. Until recently and with revisions confirmed by Vatican II the Mass could be celebrated by the priest alone, very often quite detached from the worshiper in the pew, who was either spectator or indeed preoccupied with his own private devotional practices. Not so in Orthodoxy, where the liturgy has no meaning in the private sense. Orthodoxy has managed to keep worship and theology as well as worship and evangelism together. The Orthodox view is that the presence of the church in a particular place with its liturgy *is* mission. At the heart of the Holy Liturgy is its most important part, the *Prothesis*, which may be understood as making God's intention or mission our own. As we have already observed, the Taizè community, with its emphasis both on worship and on "the mission of the presence," seems to have captured a view similar in this respect to Orthodoxy.

Worship and Mission in Methodism

But how is it with Methodists, who celebrate two hundred years in this country? In origin Methodism was not a protest movement against traditional practices of worship but, on the contrary, partly an effort to restore them. It is hard to think nowadays that once we were accused of being "sacramentarians," as well as "Bible bigots" and "enthusiasts." While John Wesley advocated frequent or weekly communion, the Bishop of London wanted the Eucharist at least once between Christmas and Pentecost! Wesley thought of Holy Communion as a "converting ordinance." In his sermon on "The Means of Grace" he regarded this service, together with prayer and the searching of Scriptures to be "ordained of God, as the ordinary channels of conveying his grace to the souls of men." He wrote in 1755 that the Anglican liturgy was "one of the most excellent human compositions that ever was." He added, though, that the Methodist societies "did not object to the use of forms, yet they dare not confine themselves to them." He himself used extempore prayer even within the formal services of the Established Church.

It was with a mind to providing the sacraments to those who otherwise would have been deprived of them that Wesley offended against Anglican discipline in ordaining several men and finally in consecrating Dr. Thomas Coke for what amounted to episcopal office. Then in September of 1784 he wrote:

And I have prepared a Liturgy little differing from that of the Church of England . . . which I advise all the travelling preachers to use on the Lord's Day in all the congregations, reading the Litany only on Wednesdays and Fridays [special days for Christians from the second century] and praying extempore on all other days. I also advise the elders to administer the Supper of the Lord on every Lord's Day.

The Christmas Conference later that same year duly, or perhaps dutifully, approved the prayer book. Asbury mentions that in 1786 he had sent a copy of it to General Washington.

Some sincere effort was made by some few preachers to follow Wesley's admonitions. Others as strongly resisted the tendency. The American preachers were roughhewn and independent. Britain and what came from her was suspect, and even the Methodists were under suspicion by the American revolutionaries because of their relation to England. Besides, formal prayers were hardly suited to the rough conditions of the circuit riders. Jesse Lee offers this explanation of "the case of the vanishing prayer book":

At this time the prayer book, as revised by Mr. Wesley, was introduced among us; and in the large towns, and in some country places, our preachers read prayers on the Lord's day: and in some cases the preachers read part of the morning service on Wednesdays and Fridays. But some of the preachers, who had been long accustomed to pray extempore, were unwilling to adopt this new plan. Being satisfied that they could pray better, and with more devotion while their eyes were shut, than they could with their eyes open. After a few years the prayer book was laid aside, and had never been used since in public worship.[2]

Thus there was set up in American Methodism a tension between order and freedom, with freedom prevailing. The more directly missionary or proclaiming elements of the liturgy came to the fore: preaching, praying, and especially the singing of hymns, though not always good ones. But these, too, are a part of liturgy,

[2] Lee, *A Short History of the Methodists* (Baltimore: Magill and Clime, 1810), p. 107.

and important parts. Recall the familiar words about John Knox: "His preaching puts more life in the bones than a thousand trumpets and five hundred drums." Wesley bequeathed to us also a genuine missionary tradition, and his phrase concerning the world as his parish— usually cited out of context—has become a kind of slogan with us. It contains a great insight, though, for "parish" literally means "beside my house," and that is where the whole world is today. We used also the love feast—a kind of lay Communion service—a development from Wesley's effort to restore the *agape* of the early church.

In a word, American Methodism spent its first hundred years getting away from formalism in worship—which was classed with the sin of worldliness—and its second hundred years by slow and painful moves toward getting back a measure of formal worship. We are not yet quite back to the point our father in the faith intended for us to be nearly two hundred years ago. There have naturally been occasional voices raised against worship that was too informal. For example, Freeborn Garretson in a sermon before the New York Conference in 1826 had these somewhat quaint words to say:

To be a lovely people, a prosperous people, a united people, people gathering all the abundant

121

harvest, we must be a holy, inoffensive people, a people following all the usages of the Church, as transmitted to us by the venerable Mr. Wesley. I say Mr. Wesley, for we all know that the Bible was his standard.

Throughout our hearts have been in the right place, for seven of our twenty-five Articles of Religion have had to do with worship, and the third portion of the General Rules also have to do with worship, as other parts have to do with mission. In the main, however, we have allowed the two to become widely separated. But worship and mission belong together.

In Bishop J. Waskom Pickett's well-known study, *Christian Mass Movements in India*, he makes the strong point that where village Christians participate in regular (preferably daily) worship and, especially, frequent Communion, there is a corresponding growth in faith, in knowledge, and in moral attainment insofar as these can be observed objectively. I repeat that worship and mission, and indeed Christian nurture, belong together.

Bringing Worship and Mission Together

Now is the time that these two, so long too much divided, must be united again in the life of the whole church. The liturgical movement

122

may well lead in this direction. I do not believe there will be a true revival of religion unless it is as a part of recovery of meaningful corporate worship. In the broad sense it may be affirmed that this has been true of all the great religious renewals of the past. Yet this will not take place by the church turning in on itself and by being preoccupied with itself in such a world as ours. Rather it must be turned inside out and become preoccupied with the world, where God's loving concern so clearly rests. And the way to do this is surely through a fresh understanding of liturgy so that it may truly, as well as literally, become a public work of God's people.

We have been at pains to argue that worship is not at odds with life but addresses itself to life. Liturgy has been rightly termed "a people's theology." If this is true, then the people must be instructed in the meaning of corporate worship—"in what goes on here." It is apparently assumed that everyone already instinctively knows the meaning of worship; and their teachers are not generally instructed to teach. Only recently have some of our seminaries offered courses in the *meaning* of corporate worship. The usual seminary course is one that might be called "liturgical engineering"—how to "construct" an order of worship, how to "build" a sermon, how to compose a pastoral prayer, how to conduct a funeral or marriage.

123

Then there have been elements of architectural engineering, too. These have been notably successful, for great numbers of our churches now have divided chancels for no other apparent reason than their supposed aesthetic appeal. While we have shown great ardor in getting an altar pushed up against the wall, we meet our Roman brethren coming in the opposite direction, putting the Lord's Table in the midst of the people, where ours—scarcely noticed—has been all along. Once again the priest can celebrate from behind the table, so recovering something of the family setting. And as for pure aesthetics, even by Kierkegaard's categories, to emphasize this is to be at least two steps removed from vital religion.

Surely all this must be corrected immediately in our seminaries so that, in turn, our people may be taught more adequately. This can be done in special groups in a local church or on occasion by a kind of "verbal rubric" within the service itself. For example, not long ago I was asked to "*give* the benediction." I seized upon the moment as one for instruction and explained that the benediction was not really a prayer but was a final word of reassurance that Christians give to one another before they part. Therefore, heads need not be bowed, but we may look our brother in the eye. Then, not the minister but the people were to say the "Amen," which is their way of voicing approval and of giving like assurance to the minister, their brother. If only we could recover the people's "Amen" at the proper places, we should have gone a long way toward liturgical recovery. Then I proceeded to say: "The grace of our Lord Jesus Christ, which is the love of God the Father, made real and present for us by the Holy Spirit, *is* yours now and always." And all the people actually said "Amen."

But there is more. Is there not a clue to meaningful worship in the Reformation phrase: "It is the chief end of man to glorify God and to enjoy him forever"? We do glorify him in the company of Christians at worship, but we need not stop there. We are to continue to glorify him and rejoice in him in the world of everydayness. Or, do we not see in Orthodoxy, which is not just "right teaching" but "right glorifying," a clue in their use of doxology? They praise him indeed in the sanctuary—and also on Main Street.

Or, is there not a kind of grand choreography in the rhythm of Christian living: a gathering as the church to worship and to be renewed in its true identity, and then a scattering as the church which has been renewed in responsibility? Within the service, in the Methodist tradition at least, there is a lesser choreography in our "going forward" to the altar for prayer and

125

Communion. Or again, can we not say that the drama of Christian living does not take place within the sanctuary? Rather, it is a rehearsal there—for we tend to forget our lines and so frequently get out of character. We have to be renewed through corporate worship to be actors in the real drama of Christian living, which is enacted in the world of everyday-ness.

So it is that some would see the liturgy as a three-act drama with prologue and epilogue in which, as I say, we are renewed with regard to our true identity and therefore with respect to our responsibility. Act I is the Service of Confession, wherein we acknowledge that we are indeed sinners but learn that we are forgiven sinners. So with real meaning we hear the invitation, "Lift up your hearts," to which we can only respond, "We lift them up unto the Lord."

This is the transition to Act II, the Service of the Word, wherein the Scriptures, conveyed to us by the community that has remembered, the community of which we are a part, are read and expounded. They assure us that we are indeed free men whose tomorrows need not be mere pale carbon copies of our yesterdays. To this we respond with our statement of loyalty, in which, in company with Christians of all ages, we confess our faith and admit that we are indeed that people whom God has delivered.

126

Again, the transition comes in a dialogue: "The Lord be with you." "And with thy spirit." "Let us pray."

Then we engage in Act III, in which we intercede for the whole world as the responsible persons we once again know ourselves to be. Finally, in offering our gifts we offer ourselves. With the final assurance of the benediction we scatter in the world to be once more the forgiven, free, responsible persons that disciples of Christ are to be. Again and again we do this, for we are a forgetful people. One of the Fathers said that our brother serves us far better than our memories.

If the service be a Communion ritual, the same realities are there in more vivid and even visible form. We are called to recollect the past; to anticipate the future; to engage meaningfully in the present as prompted by the Lord of the past, the future, and the present. But again we who have gathered in submission scatter in mission and service. For it becomes clear again that in worship we belong to God and in the world we belong to our neighbors because both they and we belong to God. For the Lord of the gathered church and of the scattered church is also, indeed first of all, the Lord of the world. In the Lord's Supper he feeds his people, but there is always bread enough and to spare. The onlooker may also see this and finally realize that Jesus Christ

127

is the host of a banquet for all mankind. Particularly they may see this if the partakers of the sacrament in the church see to it that their lives are also sacraments.

More than this, recovery of worship will come as there is recovery of its objective quality. Every time we come upon ourselves we are hiding —hiding from life. Liturgy is a re-presentation of life—it calls us back to authentic selfhood in community. Corporate worship pulls us out of ourselves. We tend to treasure our religion by an internalization or subjectivation of it. Corporate worship externalizes our focus. True worship opposes all individualization, all intellectualization, all psychologization that tries to cloak it. For we worship never merely for ourselves but as representatives of all mankind. Worship is what the whole body of Christ does for the whole world. True worship, therefore, is objective, and mission confirms the objectivity of worship through concrete obedience in the human situation. So it is that we meet Christ in worship and in human need. Karl Barth once reminded us that Christians must not go to sleep over either their Bibles or their newspapers.

We have reason to be thankful for the meeting of missionaries in Germany some years ago. They called for "permanent and radical revision of public worship." They reaffirmed the

128

corporate, rather than individualistic, nature of Christian worship and urged that once again it address itself to a real and concrete world. As if they had heard this admonition, an international group of students meeting in Wisconsin in the summer of 1965 used newspaper headlines in their daily litany. The young people gathered as a hushed congregation and with bowed heads responded "Lord have mercy upon us" as each headline was read:

"Ten thousand civil rights demonstrators marched Monday . . ." the liturgist read.

"Lord have mercy on us," the congregation replied.

"The White House raised the possibility that there will be a new military build-up in Vietnam . . ."

"Lord have mercy on us," was their response.

They saw the point, for worship and mission belong together.

129

toward
a larger
ecumenism

More than a decade ago a leading theologian observed that the encounter of the gospel with the great world religions had scarcely begun. This is an arresting assertion. Though we are still in the early stages of serious relationship, the radical and widespread meeting of the faiths is in our time a very present reality. If for the nineteenth century the great problem for the church was the relation of religion and science, then the great problem for the twentieth century may be the relations among the various religions themselves, or between the religions and the quasi-religions. Of course, there has never been a period during its long history in which this was not in some degree a problem for the church, but in our day it has reached compelling proportions and demands our urgent attention. On the other hand, it is necessary to approach this matter not as a problem but as a possibility of a larger ecumenism, embracing the vision of the unity of all mankind.

It is possible to view this subject in the more restricted sense of the new meeting within the Christian family itself. We all welcome the dramatic change in atmosphere between Roman Catholicism and the other churches. If progress is slow on the road to reconciliation between Christians of the non-Roman and Roman traditions, how much slower must the progress be in the broader perspectives of interreligious relations.

Or, again, it is possible to approach the subject from the standpoint of new Christian-Jewish relationships. In this instance one must speak with a little more reserve, for we are still only about two decades from the ruthless extermination of six million European Jews. This very fact, and the sense of guilt associated with it, prompts the Christian to find his Jewish brother in a new way. More and more, Judeo-Christian relations are seen as a part of the whole ecumenical enterprise. Our family relations would seem to demand this, for as Pope Pius XI once rightly suggested, Christians are "spiritual Jews."

It is in a setting of religious pluralism that the meeting of faiths now takes place. As a result of a great complex of factors—colonialism and its aftermath; wars and the settlements that have followed them; rapid means of travel and a rapid increase of those who travel for business or pleasure; intergovernmental activities; the reality of the United Nations; and, of course, missionary expansion—many countries are now presented with the fact of more than one religious community within their borders. We are experiencing a religious mix-up in unprecedented degree. Luther's dictum, *cujus regio, ejus religio*, no longer holds. So it is that there is currently a larger confrontation of faith with faith and of faith with unfaith than mankind has ever experienced before. The rapidly developing interdependence of peoples forces this issue upon us. All mankind is rapidly being caught up in one universal history. In the light of this, the Commission on Faith and Order of the World Council of Churches has called for a "deeper dialogue with men of other faiths." In the same meeting Professor David Cairns of Aberdeen observed that "we have been accustomed to talking of the drama of history and the drama of salvation on a normal-sized stage." We now need a larger one.

A new kind of rub of cultures has created sensitive issues of religious feeling and religious liberty. For example, not long ago a large department store in New York City displayed in one of its windows a statue of Kwannon, the Buddhist Goddess of Mercy. Purely for decorative purposes the figure was made to appear as if arrows were piercing it. Forthwith there came a protest from the Japanese Consulate General, for a visiting Japanese businessman had seen sacrilege in this display. Immediately it was removed. The other side of the coin is to be found in Japan, where department stores outdo even our own in Christmas features. One is quite at home in Tokyo during that season, for Christmas carols blare on the streets much as in an American city. Yet it seems to us offensive and even blasphemous that striptease should be offered, as it has been in Tokyo, to the tune of "Silent Night, Holy Night."

Or, once again the problem of the meeting of faiths arises in the context of religious liberty. In India, a secular state, for instance, how is a Muslim or Christian citizen to react when images of Hindu deities appear on postage stamps? Other newly formed nations are having to grapple with the meaning of a secular state and the attendant challenge of doing justice to religious minority groups within their borders. On the other hand, theocratic states such as Pakistan have a similar necessity of guaranteeing the rights of their minority of non-Muslim citizens. Furthermore, they are confronted with the need of defining what actually is meant by a

133

theocratic state. How does one conceive of an Islamic country in terms acceptable to both its liberal and conservative Muslim citizens? Yet another illustration is seen in the desperate struggle of Nepal to become a modern nation while at the same time continuing to burden itself with archaic laws that are oppressive to its religious minorities.

Of tremendous significance in the meeting of the faiths is the contemporary resurgence of traditional religions everywhere. This renaissance going on simultaneously in various traditions is stimulated by similar forces, though operative in widely separated situations. Let us briefly touch upon four of these factors.

1. The first of these is the impact upon non-Christian religions of Western culture in general and of Christianity in particular. For a long time this was an engagement between a dynamic culture and various cultures that were largely static and even dormant. For the most part the West had the upper hand and was capable, in turn, of military subjugation, political ascendancy, and economic exploitation. In the process a dormant East, where culture religions were the rule, was stabbed awake and reacted in a variety of ways—by resentment and retreat, by adoption and adaptation, by reaction and renaissance. It should be clear that where religion and culture are equated to the degree that they are in Asia,

134

an awakening of culture is an awakening of religion.

2. A second factor in the resurgence of religions is the new nationalism. Indeed, some observers have been at pains to affirm that what has taken place is not a real renaissance of religions at all, but merely a temporary reassertiveness related to nationalism. The new freedom of nearly three score nations has, in fact, been accompanied by revival of the traditional faith. I repeat that in culture religions the renewal of one aspect of life—namely, the political—is sure to register itself as a renewal in the prevailing religion of the community. The struggle for independence has meant that divergent peoples within the national borders were once united by a common animosity toward foreign rule and a common desire to be rid of it. Once independence has come, the people can no longer be held together by a union of animosity. What better alternative to effect cohesiveness than the traditional religion or traditional religious concepts? In practice this has become a powerful cement of national life.

3. Third, resurgence of traditional religions has been prompted by ethnic assertiveness. It would be entirely too simple and misleading to see this merely as a negative process. Rather, in the renaissance of religions in Asia—and in Africa—something is being affirmed concerning

the cultural values of these areas. An example would be the *Negritude* movement of West Africa. All along, Western culture as such has enjoyed far less esteem in Asia and Africa than most of us have realized or like to admit. Traditional customs and outlooks are now being set forth as replies and even alternatives to Western ways. An aspect of this may be observed especially with regard to developments in Japan. For decades she received abundantly from Western science and technology. How was self-respect to be maintained? Up to the end of the World War II, Japan's way was to endow a rather primitive and animistic popular Shinto with importance as a national symbol and rallying point. More recently Japan has spawned a number of sects of the Buddhist family, of which the Soka Gakkai may be the most notable. In one degree or another this method has been followed elsewhere: a retreat to the high and holy ground of traditional religion as a badge of self-assertion and of nationhood. This effort at face-saving and at reaffirmation of self-respect dare not be underestimated.

4. Fourth, and closely related to the last-mentioned factor, is the search for security of which the renascent religions are evidence. Men everywhere are engaged in this seeking for roots and for solid ground. The very threatened nature of the world in which we live demands this. Fear of

an unfriendly universe, anxiety about nuclear destruction, distress over moral anarchy—these are universal experiences of our day, and men in many places have turned to religion for security and solace and reassurance. The effort toward ordering of inner life when confronted with external disorder is universal. This search is not restricted to the illiterate and uneducated, but to an astonishing degree has involved the sophisticated as well. Again, men turn almost instinctively to the past securities, which traditional beliefs and practices represent, for stability in the midst of the twentieth century. Where seemingly exactly the opposite has happened—that is, where traditional religions have been suppressed or de-emphasized, as under communist rule—even there the prevailing ideology has itself become a kind of quasi-religion.

So it is that, whether it be Hinduism, Buddhism, Islam, or even animism, religions have taken on new life before our very eyes. Even as recently as a quarter of a century ago it was widely supposed that these religions were decaying or dying. Such is not the case today. They are at pains not only to reform and modernize themselves, but they have at times shown a renewed missionary impulse and now attempt to affirm their own universality.

This apologetic, polemic, and missionary thrust has for the most part taken Western

137

peoples by surprise. They have been shocked by the powerful negative reaction to their culture. While older cultures have been quite ready to receive the technical apparatus of the West, they have proved highly resistant to the presuppositions related to technology. Westerners are for the first time experiencing, by prolonged exposure to it, the resentment and resistance of other peoples. The typical Westerner is ill prepared for the present encounter. Though the specialists are better informed than ever before concerning the religions of the world, the average person is ill equipped to deal with the new problems of the meeting of faiths; for not only is he unacquainted with other faiths but he is uncertain of his own.

Though they do not lie within the central focus of this essay, mention must be made here of the secular faiths of our time that enjoy the status of quasi-religions. These may be designated in a number of ways. One of these is certainly nationalism, which frequently has religious overtones. Secularism is another. So likewise is liberal humanism, with all its ramifications in every contemporary culture. Nicolai Berdyaev and a host of other writers have made unmistakably clear the quasi-religious character of communism. The same was true of national socialism. Since more than one of these may attract the same adherent, the modern secularist may sometimes be seen as essentially poly-theistic.

These rival secular faiths are a challenge and may even be a threat to *all* religions. Whether or not we agree with the terms of his plea, the fact of the plea of India's ex-president Radhakrishnan is pertinent here:

We are living at the dawn of a new era of universal humanity. . . . We cannot base the new civilization on science and technology alone. They do not furnish a reliable foundation. We must learn to live on a new basis, if we wish to avoid the catastrophe that threatens us. We must discover the reserves of spirituality, respect for human personality, the sense of the sacred found in all religious traditions and use them to fashion a new type of man who uses the instruments he has invented with a renewed awareness that he is capable of greater things than the mastery of nature.

Our situation is this: Mankind is moving toward a more unitary culture. In this context the traditional faiths are meeting one another in an unparalleled measure. At the same time they are confronted with new quasi-religions that have no intention at all of being real religions. What shall be the response of the traditional religious communities to this new, twofold

139

situation? Particularly, what shall be the response of the church?

There is need, first of all, to clear the air of a number of matters. One of these is the notion that in relationship to religions other than one's own a stance of sentimental tolerance should be taken. This may amount to indifference to truth, which is certainly not called for if integrity is to be preserved. Karl Mannheim once wrote: "The meaning of tolerance is that everybody should have a fair chance to present his cause, but not that nobody should ardently believe his cause. This attitude of mentality in our modern democracy has gone so far that we have ceased to believe, out of mere fairness, in our own objectives." We of the West are very likely to be "soft" at this point, partly out of a sense of fairness, but partly because we are aware that anything that smacks of absolutism or intolerance is, theoretically speaking at any rate, intensely repugnant, especially to the Asian mind and indeed to modern man in general.

In this connection some note should be taken of the oft-repeated charge that Christian missionaries are particularly intolerant of religions other than their own. It is undeniable that very many of them have thoroughly deserved this judgment. On the other hand, many missionaries, both Roman Catholic and Protestant, have for centuries shown a lively and objective interest in

140

the traditional religions of the people among whom they have served. In fact, an important element in the survival and revival of these religions has been the study undertaken by or stimulated by these foreign visitors. This is often freely acknowledged by Asian scholars themselves. It was missionaries who first began a systematic study of the religions of Asia.

A word must be said also about comparative religion. There is no question about the immense debt that is owed to the multitude of able scholars who have given themselves to this important field of the science of religion. The volume of information they have collected is almost overwhelming. Insofar as knowledge is concerned, Western scholarship, at any rate, is well prepared for the meeting of faiths. These scholars have uncovered numberless parallels and convergences. The best of them have in honesty avoided the temptation of comparing the best in one religion with the worst in another. Yet, in spite of all this, comparative religion, while furthering the knowledge of religions, has not necessarily contributed to the understanding of religion. Moreover, what are the criteria by which comparisons are to be made? And how can one determine that they are correct? Moreover, the approach of comparative religions is likely to pay too little attention to the fact that the various religions are *Gestalts,*

141

experienced by their own adherents as totalities. Comparative religion has much to contribute to the debate, but it is not the means by which the problem of relationship of the faiths is to be solved.

It is tempting in thinking of the relationship of religions to turn to the syncretistic approach. Why not combine forces? There is certainly an element of syncretism as we review the history of religion, yet deliberate eclecticism has had a sad history. In the fourteenth century B.C. the Egyptian king Amenhotep IV (IKHN-ATEN) was responsible for the devising of a new religion of ethical monotheism centering in the worship of the sun deity. Though a zealous reformer, he faced great opposition from the priests of the old order. Following his death, the new religion collapsed. Caesar Augustus endeavored also to have an eclectic religion devised, but it did not long continue. The Moghul Emperor Akbar, a contemporary of Queen Elizabeth I, likewise established a new syncretistic religion called "The Divine Faith." He attempted to include as a part of it the best of Islam, Christianity, Judaism, Hindusim, Parseeism, and even atheism. This effort also collapsed after Akbar's death. Such detached and rationalistic approaches are not really live options to us. Although some syncretistic elements are natural and normal, this process takes place not under

the guidance of committees, but in the rough-
and-tumble of history.

What, then, are possible attitudes toward
faiths other than one's own? Obviously there are
many possible stances. They are likely to cluster
around one or the other of the two following
poles.

At one extreme is the common view that all
religions are essentially the same, regardless of
how they may vary in specific and superficial
detail (universalism). This is a point of view
that has found many sympathetic ears in the
Western world since the Enlightenment. It is a
viewpoint that is especially hospitable to the
Asian religions, notably Hinduism. It is put forward by Hindu apologists, such as the Vedan-
tists, almost *ad nauseam*. It is worth recalling
that Gibbon said somewhat cynically one time
that in the Roman Empire all religions were to
the people equally true; to the philosophers,
equally false; and to the government, equally
useful.

Sometimes it is said that all religions *say* the
same thing. When this is asserted it naturally
calls for an examination of precisely what they
do say and a determination of whether or not
they *are* saying the same thing. For instance, the
Hindu concept of *avatar*, or descent, and the
Christian concept of *incarnation* are superficially similar, but can it really be supported

143

that they are saying the same thing? Or does the Christian mean by *agape* the same that the Buddhist means by *karuna* (compassion)? What had Gandhi's Rama Raj to do with the kingdom of God?

This approach lends itself to many picturesque and plausible metaphors: all religions are rivers leading to the same sea; all are paths that guide one to the same mountain summit; all are islands in one great ocean; all afford a view of the same moon; the truth they treasure is one, regardless of the shape of the earthen vessel that contains it. Though this position has often been put with force and dignity, it surely leaves much to be desired. It suggests that a static situation is somehow possible or desirable. It is likely to lead to a kind of least common denominator and making everyone "an honorary member of all religions," as Dean Inge put it. It more or less settles everything in advance, so that in dialogue there is really not much to talk about. Moreover, the advocates of this position are accustomed to press it very hard, so that in the name of a wholly undogmatic approach, the assumption that all religions are the same proves itself to be a very dogmatic position indeed. It is likely to be a kind of facade for its own type of exclusivism. In New Delhi some years ago at a Congress of Religions, each speaker gave lip service to the notion that all faiths are

144

equal and then each in turn proceeded to try to show how his own religion was "more equal" than any other. Finally, this approach also tends strongly to ignore the living, indivisible unity, or *Gestalt*, of the various religious traditions. Such universalism is an inadequate starting point for the meeting of faiths. Religious search is universal; religious solutions are particular.

At the opposite pole is the position of some that only their own religion is true—an exclusivist claim. Sometimes out of modesty or a spirit of penitence for supposed arrogance we are tempted to conclude that only Christians have ever tried to uphold this position. A careful search will also reveal its presence among Hindus, Muslims, Buddhists, and others, including the quasi-religious Marxists. An instance is the fact that while we would view Islam as the religion of Muslims, a devout Muslim would regard it as the religion of God. Just as with the view that all religions are the same, so with this one; there is a presupposition implied that one has a criterion by which he can judge the validity of his position. What is this criterion and how is it authenticated? Once again conversation is cut off before it begins. Only monologue is possible. If there is no point of contact between religions, as some would aver, then only silence is possible.

It must be acknowledged that in the sweep of

145

its long history Christianity has had particular responsibility at this point. Frequently its stand has been expressed in terms that those who were not Christians were going to hell. Nicolai Berdyaev put it this way: " 'The good' are so anxious to get into the Kingdom of Heaven that in the crush at the entrance to it they are ready to trample on a great number of their neighbors and push them down to hell. . . . This is the worst defect that Christianity has suffered in human hearts." It must be observed, however, that though the exclusivist position is a kind of stereotype for the ardent religionist, there are relatively few nowadays who conform to this stereotype. William Ernest Hocking himself confessed that in spite of the fact that "radical displacement" would theoretically be one way to a world faith, the fact is that a pure advocate of this procedure is pretty hard to find. A more typical viewpoint for Christians, at any rate, would be that expressed by a sensitive missionary among Muslims that Christianity aims not at making the map more Christian but at making Christ more widely known.

There is, however, a navigable channel between the Scylla of universalism and the Charybdis of exclusivism. This is what I should like to call the confessional position. For the Christian this means he has responded to the judgment and mercy of God that have come to him in Christ. This is a matter not of acceptance of a set of principles but of acceptance of a person. It is therefore a matter not merely of belief but of surrender. It is a judgment and a commitment of faith.

By its very nature this response is exclusive for the person who is responding. It is not the mere assertion that "Jesus the Christ is Lord," which may be in itself an abstraction; it is the life-affirmation that "Jesus the Christ is *my* Lord or *our* Lord," by discovering one's self in a servant relationship to him. It is also by its very nature universal in its perspective: He who is Lord of each one is seen as Lord of all.

It goes without saying that the confessional position must be allowed to adherents of other religions also. Reinhold Niebuhr expresses this when he avers that every religious or philosophical faith is an existential commitment. We have a right to expect of advocates or witnesses of other religions that they are permitted the same utmost seriousness and fullest commitment to their faith that we would claim for ourselves.

For the Christian this is, of course, not just an individual matter. He is not only committed to his Lord as an individual but finds his place in a part of a historic community of commitment —the church. This was stated very clearly by Cardinal Mercier when he said:

The interests of a Christian are not a private matter. They are the interests of the whole community. All that you do, for good or for evil, either benefits or damages the whole society of souls. By your work, your purity of life, your participation in the common suffering, you can intensify and extend the Kingdom of Love." [1]

As a part of this corporate structure, the Christian has a responsibility of confessing his faith in the world. This he understands not just as his mission in the world but as his involvement in what God is doing in the world. He confesses to the faithfulness of God, which demands a faithfulness on his own part in response. This confession is not understood as mere propaganda or pressure or passion for another person to change his religious affiliation. It would invite and persuade, not compel. It is a joyful sharing of the news of what great things God has done for all men as these are encountered in Jesus the Christ. Moreover, the Christian has the responsibility of witness regardless of response to it or results.

Surprisingly enough, the confessional position is in reality not one of bondage but one of freedom. It is not one of arrogance but one of profound humility. It need not be an assertion of

[1] Cited by A. C. Bouquet, *The Christian Faith and Non-Christian Religions* (New York: Harper & Bros., 1958), p. 415.

superiority, but is a constant summons to repentance on the part of the witness himself. It testifies to the mercy and judgment of God upon one's self as well as upon all men. Nor is it restrictive to the point of blinding one to the truth and grace that have been experienced in other commitments of faith. This confession is not an assurance of fullest attainment, but it is a constant judgment upon our failure to attain.

The confessional position does offer a place for one to stand, so that he knows where he stands. It affords also a stance from which to view and converse with other faiths. This conversation must be done with an openness that is achieved in the delicate balance between commitment to one's own faith and a refusal to accept with complacence the religious status quo in our world, which may be implied by religious pluralism.

Basic to such an openness is *respect* for religions other than one's own, or better, respect for their adherents. For, as William Temple helpfully observed: "Whatever thought any human soul is seeking to live by, deserves the reverence of every other human soul." This all men would desire for themselves; it is the least they owe to others. As one who has lived for considerable periods in Asian countries, I can testify to the courtesy I have received in this regard. I do not know of any more moving instance of this quality than that shown a century ago by Cardinal Lavigerie of Algiers. It was his practice when passing a mosque to get out of his carriage and walk past barefooted.

Furthermore, such openness involves a readiness for objective study of other religions. The attachment to one's own faith as a Christian embraces also a kind of detachment—a readiness to take risks, even the readiness to be tempted to leave one's own spiritual heritage for another. In other words, there needs to be a readiness for what someone has called an open shop in our contemporary study of the world's religions.

Fundamental to all this is the acknowledgment that we have much to learn from one another—in fact, have learned much. Is this not one of God's ways of teaching us? So it is that we may learn from the African something of vitality and the depths of humanness; from the Chinese, a fuller order in human relations; from the Hindu, greater depth of inwardness. From outstanding personalities of other faiths we can learn something of our shortcomings with respect to the practice of our own faith.

There would appear to be ample scriptural sanction for the openness of which I speak. While it is true that in the Old Testament there is a tension between nationalism and universalism, the later prophets speak forth for one

God who is Lord of all. The Bible has little to say of other religions as such, but it tells of a God who is available to all men, for "the whole earth is full of his glory."

In the Gospels it is scandalous the way in which Jesus turns to non-Jewish people as models of faith and conduct. We readily miss the real force of the parable of the good Samaritan or the ten lepers, in both of which a hated Samaritan is the hero. This is very much like recommending the late Dr. Martin Luther King, Jr., as an exemplar to a member of a White Citizens' Council. This same Jesus of Nazareth announced that he had come not to abolish the law and the prophets but to fulfill them. "Not every one who says to me, 'Lord, Lord,' shall enter the kingdom of heaven, but he who does the will of my Father who is in heaven." In similar vein he reminds his hearers that those who do good may not always be aware that they do it for his ake. Such is the one who was seen as "a light for revelation to the Gentiles." So much for the Synoptic Gospels.

It is the Fourth Evangelist who, *par excellence*, sets forth the universal Christ as the true light that enlightens every man. He it was who spoke of God loving the whole world through his son, of a God who seeks man. Here we find these words on the lips of the Christ: "I am the light of the world"; "I have other sheep, that are not of this fold"; "In my Father's house are many rooms." It is the Fourth Evangelist who presents the gospel in the terms of the needs of every man in his everydayness—the hungry, thirsty, lame, blind, rootless, the dead. Here is the most existential gospel—for all men.

Glancing at Paul's writings for only a moment we find him asking: "Is God the God of Jews only? Is he not the God of the Gentiles also?" Then he answers his own query: "Yes, of the Gentiles also." In another setting we hear him say that in Christ all the promises of God find their "Yes." There is no reason to restrict this "Yes" to only one tradition. It bids us, therefore, to be open to all men; or, more than that, that all men be open to one another.

For the Christian who enters into dialogue there is a long heritage of ways of relating his faith with other faiths. One of the most impressive is the *logos* doctrine, seized upon by the Fourth Evangelist. Here a contemporary term of long and complex history, denoting the self-expression of the divine, is identified with Jesus, the Christ. Throughout Christian history and down to the present day there have been those theologians who have seen this as the chief bridge to other faiths. Once again, Christ is seen at work hiddenly in all faiths. Hear William Temple while he says:

152

All that is noble in non-Christian systems of thought or conduct or worship is the work of Christ upon them and within them. By the word of God, that is to say, by Jesus Christ—Isaiah, and Plato and Zoroaster and Buddha conceived and uttered such truths as they declared. There is only one divine light; and every man in his measure is enlightened by it.[2]

So it is that every truth is clarified in the light of Christ.

Or again, the Holy Spirit is seen as operative among all men and the guide of the church to fuller truth. Professor Hocking had this to say of the matter:

It is peculiar to Christianity that in its view revelation is progressive and unfinished: this is one of the meanings of the Holy Spirit, the perpetual contemporaneousness, personalness, and novelty of the unfolding of the meaning of its truth. No one who declines to admit that form of change which means the arrival of new light—"He shall guide you into all truth"—has understood this doctrine.

As the Holy Spirit is uniquely present in Christ and, by extension, in the church, the Holy Spirit is universally present throughout the cosmos.

Others would view Everyman seeking that reality poetically designated as the light, the

[2] Temple, *Readings in St. John's Gospel* (London: Macmillan & Co., 1952), p. 10.

way, the door, the bread of life, and what is called in our tradition "Messiah." This that he seeks is offered to him in the One whom Christians confess as Christ. Yet others have seen in Christianity, and more specifically in Christ, the fulfillment of every religious aspiration and of all religions. Someone has expressed it picturesquely: "The pre-Christian religions were the age-long prayer. The Incarnation was the answer." Still others see Christianity not as a religion in the usual sense, although it undoubtedly has its cultural dimension, but as a gospel offering judgment and redemption to all mankind, including those who are in the church. The gospel is thus not a religion alongside other religions, but the end of religion. The contrasting perspective is set forth strikingly in Genesis. Man's illusory initiative is seen in Genesis 11:4, "let us make a name for ourselves"; while Genesis 12:2 speaks of the initiative of God, "I will make of you a great nation." The gospel is a self-understanding and an understanding of the universe. Or, Christianity may be seen related to other faiths in an awareness of common humanity, particularly at a time when life upon earth is itself at stake. We may speak not so much of "radical displacement" as of "regenerating, transforming incorporation."

Undoubtedly one or another of these views offers great confidence and security to the Chris-

154

tian as he seeks to live in our kind of world in which geography has ceased to offer boundaries for faiths. A similar exercise on the part of adherents to other faiths is certainly open to them —that is, to consider how their religion relates effectively to those of alien faith. It must be admitted, however, that all such "in-the-family" talk may not easily convince those who are outside the family. The case must, as ever, be established in a harsh and skeptical world. For in the marketplace of the world only the inherent merit of an idea or ideal carries weight and commends itself to others.

Love always seeks to communicate; finally, then, dialogue between the adherents must take place, and indeed is constantly taking place. Sometimes this is through the medium of well-equipped scholars and official representatives of the various religions and on a formal basis. Sometimes it is as a part of the deliberate activity of the missionaries of one or another tradition. More often it is the chance and informal interchange in the marketplace by ordinary people. Increasingly it is and can be planned for quite specifically by the church—the church that is willing to *be* the church as the "Christ-centered, Christ-inspired and Christ-obeying community." One would expect other religious traditions to be themselves, for surely truth and integrity are not served by pretending, in seeming

generosity but actually relying on defensive lati-
tudinarianism, already to possess every insight of
all other traditions.

Effective dialogue presupposes a number of
things on the part of the Christian faith, for
which alone a Christian can in some sense speak.
First of all, there must be an assumption that
the same God who has prompted us has also
prepared our counterpart for dialogue. I know,
of course, that this assumption is full of problems for many people, but without it is any
conversation possible at all? Second, it must be
assumed that all religious men are prompted by
some sense of the presence of God to whom they
respond in worship. As John Baillie says: "Of
such a Presence it must be true that to those
who have never been confronted with it, argu-
ment is useless; while to those who have, it is
superfluous." Third, there must be an assumption of some basis for interchange, for clarifica-
tion, for mutual understanding of the other's
position. It does not necessarily imply that
mutual agreement need be reached.

In any event it must be acknowledged that
religions are changing. They are really met not
in textbooks but in people. The meeting of
faiths does not so much take place in the realm
of ideas. The meeting of real people in real life
is the true point of contact between two religions. We will have to face them as they are

and as they claim to be. Nor will the Christian or any other adherent dictate the terms of the encounter, or set the examination paper, as someone has put it, to insure that he will get a good mark. How difficult and prolonged the process of dialogue is likely to be is seen by considering the degrees of difficulty involved in ever-widening boundaries of confrontation: Protestant with Protestant; Protestant with Roman Catholic or Eastern Orthodox; Christian with Jew; Judeo-Christian with Muslim; Semitic with non-Semitic; and all these with the quasi-religious.

But this process *is* going on. Recently, for example, near the University City in Paris where are housed six thousand students from eighty countries, the World Council of Churches helped to establish a "house of dialogue." We all are aware of other areas of intercourse. Such a process requires great patience and listening if each is to linger with the other long enough for mutual comprehension to take place. For comprehension and not compromise is the first necessity. Hear what Kenneth Cragg has to say about this:

For what then, on the Christian side, does the situation call? For a stout-heartedness that refuses to be daunted, a patient travail in interpretation, a will to explore humbly with thinking men of every faith

157

on none the meanings of Christ, and a quality of life that compels men to "stay for an answer" and leaves them in no doubt as to where it lies.

In quite another context Cragg suggests the proper mood of the Christian in dialogue. Not, "We have the truth; sit down and listen while I tell it to you!" But rather: "We Christians have found in Jesus Christ the wonder of God as Love. Shall we talk of it together?"

Dialogue implies always the frankest and fullest interchange. Each is surely responsible to truth as he sees it. For the Christian is convinced that his faith illuminates the truth about God and man; about God's identification of himself with man's sin and struggle; about freedom and responsibility; about man's inner needs and the demands of social justice; about the demands of righteousness and the grace of forgiveness. Sometimes opposition and hostility will arise. Then relevance is likely to be present. For men do not oppose what does not concern or offend them. The ends of truth must be served, but for the Christian this is under the Holy Spirit, who, he believes, will lead men to all truth. Conversion in the usual sense cannot be the aim of dialogue, for that is in the hands not of men but of God. Conversion may, however, be the result of dialogue. If this be true, then both parties must be open to conversion to insights neither has hitherto known. Perhaps the most reassuring fact is that in many quarters of the world precisely this sort of thing is going on. Very sensitively this is taking place in the Middle East between Christians and Muslims. In a new sense an encounter between Christians and Hindus in India is in process. Japan is practically a laboratory of religions and conversations take place constantly among religious leaders there. In all candor, though, it must be acknowledged that save for Japan, other nations of the East are not at present producing very many advocates of their traditional religions competent to engage in scholarly dialogue.

Paul Tillich, during his last years, shared an account of "A Christian-Buddhist Conversation." [3] He testified as to both the seriousness and anxiety involved. Furthermore, he pointed out that such conversation must make "unceasing reference to the quasi-religions and their secular background. In this way the dialogue loses the character of a discussion of dogmatic subtleties and becomes a common inquiry in the light of the world situation, and it may happen that particular theological points become of secondary importance in view of the position of

[3] Cf. *Christianity and the Encounter of the World Religions* (New York: Columbia University Press, 1963), pp. 53 ff.

defense of all religions proper." He then described very movingly how a particular conversation must come to a preliminary end. But he continued by suggesting that religions may break through their particularities. When this is done, a religion is in a position to speak to the meaning of existence that all men seek.

The meeting of faiths suggests this approach: commitment, openness, conversation. Then perhaps dialogue will become witness. We need not be under strain that one particular point of view must prevail, or that all contribute their most precious insights for a new mixture, or that religion will disappear. An unseemly anxiety to preserve our heritage is to lose it and, at the same time, to attempt to limit God; but a willingness finally to risk even the loss of our heritage in the service of God and man is to find it. When there is a readiness to risk all, God may be trusted to be faithful in giving all back again in a renewed and enlarged perspective. Where exactly he is leading us we cannot know, but the man of faith has always been prepared to set out for an unknown destination. Nevertheless, those who begin dialogue knowing themselves to be prompted in all their beginnings by the One who is the Beginning may confidently expect that at the destination they will encounter this same One, who is also the End.